THE POWER OF
EMOTION

Also by Michael Sky

Breathing: Expanding Your Power and Energy

THE POWER OF
EMOTION

Using Your
Emotional Energy
to Transform Your Life

MICHAEL SKY

Bear & Company
Rochester, Vermont

Bear & Company
One Park Street
Rochester, Vermont 05767
www.InnerTraditions.com

Bear & Company is a division of Inner Traditions International

Copyright © 2002 by Michael Sky

Library of Congress Cataloging-in-Publication Data
Sky, Michael, 1951-
  The power of emotion : using your emotional energy to
transform your life / Michael Sky.
      v. cm.
Includes bibliographical references.
Contents: 1. Dancing with fire — 2. Energy in motion — 3.
Emotional suppression —
4. The costs of suppression — 5. Flow — 6. Love — 7. Relational
inheritance — 8. Social viruses — 9. Healing relationship — 10. A
happy childhood — 11. Living creatively.
  ISBN 1-879181-92-4
  1. Emotions. I. Title.

BF531 .S59 2003
152.4—dc21   2002013159

Printed and bound in the United States at Capital City Press

10 9 8 7 6 5 4 3 2 1

This book was typeset in Stone serif, with Lucida sans as a
display typeface

for Xiaowen

Contents

Acknowledgments

With Gratitude:

to Penny and Xiaowen for their love, inspiration, and all the quiet mornings;

to Gay Hendricks, Peggy Dylan, Mike White, Alice Miller, Gary Craig, Andrew Bard Schmookler, Leonard Orr, and Anna Coy for insightful nudges in new directions;

to Monica Woefel for gently shaping the early manuscript;

to Marilyn McGuire for the great support she's given me and so many other writers;

to Susan Davidson and Dana Walsh for helpful edits, and artist Alex Grey and designer Greg Crawford for a brilliant cover;

to Masumi Hori, Voice, and all my Japanese friends and students who invited me into their special world of emotion;

and, especially, to Adi Da Samraj, living master and teacher extraordinaire. Over the past twenty-five years, I have derived always clear guidance and happy crazy wisdom from his steady flow of amazing books.

Introduction

The bodily being of Man is constantly sustained by the Eternal, All-Pervading Force of Life. In our infantile recoil, reaction, and psycho-physical contraction toward self, we separate from the Eternal Reality and become self-possessed. Thus, we begin to starve and suffer. . . . If only the body-mind will open into the Current of Radiant Life, with full feeling and without thought, it will be liberated from the self-possessed games of tension and release of tension. Then there is only Fullness of Life.

—Adi Da Samraj, *The Eating Gorilla Comes in Peace*

What a muddle we make of our emotions. From an early age we struggle to hold back tears, to rein in temper, to stifle fear. We worry about the future and regret the past. We ache from loneliness but recoil from intimacy. We want and we want, and so much of our wanting goes unfulfilled, leaving us frustrated, ashamed, envious. Our lives reveal a myriad of ways to feel bad; we feel bad much of the time.

Yet even feeling good brings difficulties. Pleasure leads easily into lust, as success leads into pride and appreciation, into greed. Love hurts as surely as it heals. Over-enthusiasm causes various problems, as do laughing too loudly and playing too hard. Faith begets betrayal, joy begets disappointment, and sex begets major complications. The good feelings never seem to last, and the more urgently we enjoy them, the more their passing wounds us.

Over time most people develop strategies for feeling *less*. Since emotion vexes and torments us so, we find ways to suppress our emotional experience. We learn to deaden our feelings, to turn off sensation, to numb out. Like rocks in the midst of rushing water—unmoved and unmovable—we cultivate stoicism. We strive to prevail, unaffected by life's changes. Those who never show their feelings reap the highest praise.

We rationalize. Emotional expression belongs to the world of children, we say, while maturity means getting one's emotions under control. The overly emotional seem weak under fire; we favor those who remain firm and clearheaded during the worst of times. We especially spurn the messiness of emotional display, its bad form and awkward timing. Spiritual advancement, we assume, requires the taming of one's feelings. We distrust decisions and actions that have too much emotional influence. We try to do things rationally and logically, to act without feeling.

Ultimately each of us finds our own way with emotion. Some people—the granite faced and stone hearted—manage to completely suppress their feelings. Most only partially succeed: one never cries, for instance, but melancholy persists. Other people utterly fail despite all efforts, therapies, and medications; they spend their lives in a psychiatric soup of mutinous emotion. Still others ignore all of society's warnings and antiemotional dictates and remain unabashedly romantic, zealous, fiery, gushy, sentimental: they become artists, musicians, eccentrics, or clowns and migrate to the margins of social respectability.

Being socially acceptable demands that we get our feelings under firm control and keep emotional energy mostly unexpressed. That so many people do so well at suppressing their emotions constitutes a singular failing in human development and, I believe, a root cause of many problems of modern society.

Since the mid-1970s I have been meeting with individuals and groups as a therapist, counselor, teacher, and bodyworker. I have listened to thousands of life stories and have worked with a wide range of physical and psychological symptoms and complaints. I have learned that emotion plays an essential role in our lives, for better and for worse; that emotional energy subsists as a vital force within the human organism and as the functional link between body, mind, spirit, and environment; and that flowing with one's feelings opens the way to physical health, mental clarity, greater success in relationships, and more effective creativity.

I define emotion as *energy-in-motion.* Like ocean waves undulating along a shoreline, emotional energy exists as a constant flowing presence in our lives. Human feelings—these subtle currents, part liquid, part electric—arise as vital energy moving within, around, and between us, forever animating spirits, coloring thoughts, influencing dreams, heartening relationships, and providing the raw material for our bodies and creative efforts.

This book describes a radical path to *Homo emotus:* the feeling human. You will learn first to actively accept your emotions; second, to keep your emotional energies in perpetual motion; and finally, to direct all emotions to good, creative use. You will learn four basic tools that will profoundly transform your emotional experience. With time you can effectively marshal the creative force that dwells in every feeling.

At the end of each chapter I have included simple breathing practices that help you to experience and develop your energy-in-motion. I recommend that you do each practice at least once (the more the better), that you do them *as you read*, and that you do them in the order they appear in the book. In this way you will develop, step by step, an awareness of your breathing as an ever present and always flowing transformational process. By the end of *The Power of Emotion*, if you have practiced you will possess powerful tools for improving your physical and mental health, your relationships, and your creative efforts. Moreover, you will have formed a lasting appreciation for the beauty and power of human emotion.

1

Dancing with Fire

At our most elemental, we are not a chemical reaction, but an energetic charge. Human beings and all living things are a coalescence of energy in a field of energy connected to every other thing in the world. This pulsating energy field is the central engine of our being and our consciousness, the alpha and the omega of our existence.

—LYNN MCTAGGART, *THE FIELD*

In the Kalahari Desert of central South Africa live an ancient people called the Kung. For the past several thousand years the Kung have lived a simple nomadic existence, following water about the desert and filling their days with the basic pleasures of gathering and sharing food, raising children, and joining in a variety of community rituals and celebrations.

Every month or so the Kung come together for their most important community ritual, the firedance. They build a large stack of wood and set it aflame, and then they begin to dance around the fire. Some of the people drum, others sing, and

5

the strongest members of the community dance and dance, for hours and hours. They dance for so long and so vigorously that their dancing feet dig a groove in the earth surrounding the fire. As the dancing goes on, a shared feeling of excitement grows within the whole group, building and escalating, even as the fire, once furious, gradually quiets.

Then the moment arrives and the firedance begins. One dancer spins into the fire, followed by another, and then others. The dancers twirl and leap upon the glowing coals. They bend to touch the fire's flame with their fingers and sometimes with their faces and hair. They scoop up handfuls of the red-hot embers and shower them over their heads and bodies. They rub burning coals into their flesh. Sometimes they swallow live coals. Through it all they dance and dance: they dance with the fire, as the fire dances with them. Eventually the dancing slows and comes to a close, the fire spent and cooling, the dancers likewise wearily fulfilled. Within the whole community there hums a feeling of quiet celebration and powerful healing.

While many cultures around the world share a tradition of firedancing, the Kung take the practice to extraordinary lengths. And while for many other cultures firedancing seems forever veiled in mystery and supernaturalism, the Kung have a simple explanation for how it works—how humans can bring flesh into contact with extreme heat and experience joy and healing rather than pain and burning.

According to the Kung, we live in a world imbued with a great creative spirit—a vital, living energy—that they call *num*. They experience num as a luminous force that fills and surrounds the body, regulates the body's organs and governs its processes, and, under certain conditions, empowers a person to perform extraordinary activities, such as spontaneous healing, mental telepathy, clairvoyance, and dancing on hot coals. The Kung's experience of num bears close resemblance to the Chinese *chi* and the yogic *prana*, to the Japanese *ki*, the Hawaiian *mana*, the African *voodoo*, and the Christian *spirit*, as well as to Reich's *orgone*, Mesmer's *animal magnetism,* and Hippocrates' *physis*. Indeed, throughout time and place innumerable cultures have known this vital energy that fills and surrounds us and serves as a source of power in our daily lives.

The Kung say that when a person's num "boils over"—when it builds, flows, and expands vigorously—then the person's energy and the energy of the fire come together in a beneficial way, and flesh may contact fire without injury. But when a person's num contracts negatively—turning weak, cold, sickly, tight, unfocused—then his or her energy offers no protection, and the fire will burn. The state of one's num determines the creative possibilities and limits of one's body and mind. Boiling energy—building, flowing, and expanding num—empowers a person to his or her fullest potential as a creative being.

For all their history of firedancing the Kung never take the experience for granted. Sometimes, for some dancers, the experience does go badly, resulting in serious burns. Every Kung dancer accepts as a law of nature that fire burns; everyone knows that getting burned while firedancing looms as an ever-present danger. Accordingly, most firedances begin with a strong feeling of apprehension pulsing through the group. At times, especially for first-time dancers, or when a recent experience of a bad burn still lingers in memory, the apprehension can build into fear and even terror.

Yet such fears rarely stop the dancers. Rather, the Kung have learned to turn their fears into the boiling num of joyful dancing. Firedancing has taught the Kung—and could teach us—that fear arises before a firedance as the very stuff and substance of a successful experience; that the quivering, shaking, and often uncontrollable vibrating that dancers feel as their time to dance approaches all occur as manifestations of num, of vital energy spontaneously arising within and boiling, or expanding, toward empowered action; that fear exists not as some abstract bogey-force or personal flaw, but as a tangible energy moving for a creative purpose.

The Kung firedancers challenge all of us to accept fear as a spontaneous and purposeful movement of vital energy. Fear-energy moves within us in response to specific situations and events. Fear-energy arises as needed—when we feel threatened or challenged—as the motive force and raw material for an effective response.

For instance, if a large growling tiger comes into the room, you will immediately experience a strong rush of energy, which will in turn trigger a series of physiological reactions—quickening heartbeat, faster breathing, surging adrenaline, sharpening senses, tensing muscles—all of which occur as spontaneous preparation for an empowered response to the perceived threat. Classically, we think of two responses: fight or flight. You perceive the tiger, fear-energy rushes through you, and your body automatically reacts by fighting with fear-driven intensity or by running away with fear-driven speed. Other possible responses do exist: you might leap in front of another person to protect him or her from the tiger; you might find a way to meaningfully communicate with the tiger; you might beatifically surrender to the tiger's attack. However you respond, you will experience success or fulfillment to the degree that you use the fear-energy inherent in the moment.

The perceived threat causes the arousal of fear-energy, which empowers an effective response. We show such exquisite design, really; without the creative power of fear-energy, humanity would have succumbed to the tigers aeons ago.

As another example, consider that bane of modern existence: money-related stress. While a sudden catastrophic change in one's financial reality might cause the exact same energetic-physiological response as a sudden growling tiger, for most people persistently tight money causes a quiet but all too persistent mental anxiety or physical tension, or both. Anxiety and tension—fear's quieter cousins—occur as similar movements of life-energy in response to perceived threats. For the individual beset with financial problems, the tense and anxious feelings might serve as the fuel to work harder, create a more austere lifestyle, gain fresh insight into one's relationship with money, or make a major career change or cross-country move; they might be the driving spirit of the pioneer, inventor, and entrepreneur. We can try in vain to just stop feeling so stressed about money, or we can tap in to the strong energies of money-related stress and channel them toward effective response.

Notice that any perceived threat might cause the arousal of fear-energy. This includes irrational fears, when the object of our fear does not actually threaten us and may not even exist. The entirely real fear-energy generated by such fabricated threats nonetheless arises as the stuff of effective response. The person who worries incessantly about an impending invasion of giant bloodthirsty bunny rabbits generates the energy of a psychological breakthrough or spiritual crisis, or perhaps the energy to motivate a trip to a therapist or to attract the intervention of close friends. Ignoring such "unreal" fears rarely works because the all too real fear-energy they generate will find resolution—one way or another.

The person who discovers a lump in the body and falsely imagines a growing cancer may generate the very same anxious, death-obsessing feelings as those of someone who truly has cancer. For each person, the anxious feelings arise as the motive force and raw material for effective response to a perceived threat. For each person, a successful outcome will depend on the degree to which he or she successfully uses the emotional energies generated by the threat. Conversely, a poor outcome invariably befalls the one who poorly uses his or her fear-energy, however real or unreal the perceived threat.

Life ever changes, and many of life's changes confront and challenge us. Those changes that we perceive as threatening (to the body, family, livelihood, home, religion, country, planet) will trigger feelings of fear, anxiety, and tension. Such feelings forever arise as gifts of vital energy—the creative power needed to successfully deal with whatever happens.

— ◄O► —

Always Moving Breath

Now, even as you read, bring attention to the movement of your breath.

Notice that you can read these words and make sense of their meaning,

While at the same time you can pay attention to the movement of your breath.

As best you can, let your breath become one continuous flowing motion.

Breathing in through the nose, allow a slow easy inhale, filling your torso,

And just as you feel full, without stopping or holding,

Release the breath out through the nose, a long easy exhale,

And just as you feel empty, without stopping or holding,

Breathe in again, a slow easy inhale, and just as you feel full,

Breathe out again, a long easy exhale, until you feel empty,

And breathe in again, the breath always moving,

And breathe out again, the breath always moving,

One continuous breath, gentle and fluid, always moving, always flowing,

Always moving, always flowing, always moving, always breathing. . . .

2

Energy in Motion

Energy is now our common ground. As human matter we vibrate, the control panels we call our brain systems vibrate, and our whole brain-mind-body vibrates. We are energy beings. This is even more descriptive of us and our potential future than saying we are human beings.

—Elaine De Beauport, *The Three Faces of Mind*

As we experience fear, so we experience the other emotions. All of our emotions manifest as moving (arising, vibrating, gathering, flowing, expanding, boiling) energy. When we have a feeling—any feeling—we experience a tangible movement of vital energy. The energy moving through us comprises the feeling; such energy-in-motion *is* emotion.

Just as fear-energy arises in response to specific perceptions, likewise does the full range of human emotion. Each of us perceives life's changes in our own way; we then spontaneously generate emotional energy as the motive force for effective response. We perceive reality and then emotionally respond to our perceptions. Our success and failure in life, our happiness and unhappiness, derive largely from how we deal with the constant flux of emotional energies.

When what we want in a situation corresponds with what actually happens, then we tend to experience the energy moving within us as positive emotion. Quite simply, we *feel good*. The good feeling comes from our acceptance of what happens, including the present movement of vital energies. We feel good—we are happy—in those moments when we readily accept the movement of life, including the moving energy of our emotional-creative process.

Our more positive emotions arise as variations of feeling good. Joy, peace, faith, trust, hope, devotion, commitment, inspiration, ecstasy, affection, compassion, love: each occurs as a tangible movement of vital energy that pleases us (feels pleasurable) as we accept our immediate perception of reality. The more that we can accept—ourselves and other people, circumstances and events—the more positively enjoyable and creatively supportive our emotional energies become.

As an example, the moment that one person perceives another as sexually attractive, a strong current of pleasurable sexual energy starts churning within and boiling outward as a creative-attractive force toward the other person. Moving sexual energy feels good: it motivates future action, and it serves as the tangible stuff of creative response. If both people enjoy the unfolding situation—if their perceptions of reality agree with what they want—then the energy will intensify, cause more pleasure, and motivate them both toward closer contact. When the two finally touch, the living energy within each body pleasurably explodes, expands outward, and envelops the other. If both continue to accept and move with the energies they will experience the most exquisite of emotional movements—sexual intercourse and orgasm—and will cocreate, perhaps, a deepening intimacy between two people. They may even create a new human being.

All of our positive emotions operate in more or less the same way. They occur as movements of vital energy in support of our creative purpose and process, as well as moment-to-moment indicators of our actual progress in life. For most of our lives, *feeling good* should function as the primary emotional-energetic matrix out of which we perceive reality and choose to act. The more we embrace our positive emotions, the more healthy, creative, and successful we will become.

Our more negative emotions occur when we fail to accept whatever happens, including our energy-in-motion. If you receive news that somebody you care for deeply has died, you will likely experience a surge of emotional energy, especially in the upper chest, called sadness. Sadness-energy arises as a healthy response to a perceived and immediately unacceptable loss. It makes sense to feel sad when you experience loss, just as, most often, crying helps; tears can effect an energetic cleansing of undelivered communications, of missed opportunities, of disquieting memories, of interrupted dreams. Through crying, you move this sadness-energy to wash free the unfinished concerns of an important relationship. The intense grieving that follows a great loss comes as a blessing balm, a healing salve, and as the creative power that enables you to accept, let go, and move on.

Even minor losses generate some sadness-energy. The sadness that a sports fan feels when his or her team loses the big game might serve as the energy of detaching from and caring less about such things in the future, as can the sadness we feel when a celebrity dies, or when we ruin a favorite sweater in the wash. Sadness can form the foundation of one's compassion: those who accept their own feelings of grief have the most to offer others in pain. And sadness often opens a bridge to understanding, a feeling-wave that brings us closer to others and allows us to share intimacy, caring, and love.

Now consider anger. We typically feel angry when we perceive an unacceptable violation of our self-interests—which encompasses our bodies, families, communities, and nations, our legal rights, our religions and beliefs, our dreams and aspirations, and most anything else in which we have strongly invested. Anger-energy arises when we perceive that somebody or something has violated a vital element of our world. Like fear and sadness, anger occurs not as a mistake or sign of weakness; rather, anger empowers us to respond effectively to the immediately unacceptable violations of life.

Too often we use anger-energy to fight. We feel violated and strong anger-energy escalates within, providing the power to attack the perceived violator. In the case of a just war, or of a justified defense against a violent assault, anger can indeed motivate a person to fight and further the possibility of success.

Yet using anger-energy to attack others rarely works since those we attack will typically feel violated in turn and will naturally experience an expansion of anger-energy. Thus they will return the attack and violate again and stimulate more anger in us, and on and on. Ironically, such cycles of violence, though terrible in themselves, feed on the generation and expansion of intrinsically healthy life-energy and can fuel a potentially effective response to perceived violations. We avoid the cycle of violence not by making anger go away, but by finding better ways to use its powerful energies.

Anger-energy works best when channeled toward meaningful communication. The legal systems of civilized cultures involve complex processes of communication devised essentially to deal with anger; the adversarial anger that underlies most legal proceedings shows that the "rule of law" does not eliminate anger-energy but tries to manage it in more productive ways than interpersonal violence. Nonviolent conflict resolution, conflict mediation, and the Gandhian way of peaceful resistance all developed as modern refinements of the practice of transforming anger-energy into effective communication. For those who have learned how to communicate through their anger and to listen to the anger of others, anger-energy can lead to the resolution of conflicts and foster the necessary awareness to avoid future violations.

Anger-energy also serves as the fuel for hard work and peak performances. "Success is the best revenge": when somebody violates your self-interest, feel all of the anger-energy boiling within and do something. In every gym, factory, and corporate office a significant amount of what gets accomplished results from people working off their anger. Similarly, we can learn to direct anger-energy inward for the work of self-transformation. The best solution to a perceived violation may entail a major change of heart or a conversion to a whole new way of looking at things. Anger-energy can provide both the incentive and the staying power for such profound breakthroughs and transformations.

Fear, sadness, and anger arise as essential aspects of human existence. Rather than try to make these feelings go away, we can learn to use their living energies to respond effectively and creatively to the always-changing play of our lives.

All of our other more negative emotions energetically derive from fear, sadness, and anger (as the color spectrum derives from three primary colors), and they all operate in the same way. Hate, shame, guilt, jealousy, envy, lust, greed—each arises as a distinct current of vital energy moving in response to a perceived problem and offering a possible solution. We move forward in life not by avoiding such emotions but by finding ways to successfully spend their potent energies.

We feel hatred toward those whom we have judged as most unlike ourselves (often because of perceived violations).

Hate-energy can show us the way to forgive our trespassers, to surrender to that which unites all people, to discover the wisdom of tolerance, to embrace diversity.

We feel shame when we perceive our own actions as dishonorable, disgraceful, or greatly disappointing in the eyes of others. Shame-energy can help to strengthen the personal will and direct it along a path of right action.

We feel guilty when we perceive ourselves as responsible for some wrongdoing. Guilt-energy can bring clear insight into our past actions and early emotional influences and can serve as a powerful guide to self-awareness and self-understanding.

Jealousy mixes a fear of being excluded with anger over another's love or success. We best direct jealousy-energy inward to nurture the experience of self-love and self-affirmation.

We feel envious when we desire the qualities or possessions of another. Envy-energy teaches us to be the source of our own happiness.

Lust and greed arise as powerful currents of desire-energy. Each reveals weakness and helps us to become better focused in our desires.

From moment to moment each of us must personally discern the nature of unfolding events and of the energies moving within, and then chart our own course of action. In coming chapters we will learn more about different emotional energies and how to best utilize their movements. We begin by accepting that all emotions serve as vital and potentially glorious parts of being human.

Once we understand the emotions as quantities of vital energy with great potential for creativity and healing, then we can no longer think in terms of an absolutely positive or negative emotion. The full range of human emotions—from bloodcurdling fear to soul-singing joy—comprises a spectrum of living energy moving in creative response to specific perceptions. Our overall experience of any emotion derives from uniquely personal and ever-changing factors. Fear-energy can tighten into a knot of tension and worry, or it can boil over into excitement and the power to act. Love-energy offers the most sublime and nurturing of human feelings, yet love can also contract into bitterness and regret. Our experience of an emotion as positive or negative always flows from our unique perceptions and chosen responses.

Rather than *negative* and *positive,* we can use the terms *difficult* and *easy* to describe our immediate experience of any emotion, depending on our level of acceptance of the situation and of the emotion itself. We can think of *using* emotional energy *poorly* or *well,* depending on what we actually do with its inherent energies.

Since we rarely immediately accept the threats, losses, and violations in our lives, the emotions that we tend to think of as negative do indeed give us the most difficulty. We experience such emotions as difficult precisely because of our inability or unwillingness to accept our immediate reality. The emotional energies struggle to move within a psychoenergetic matrix of refusal, resistance, and denial. Our more difficult emotions arise as the motive force for effective response to immediately unacceptable situations; such emotions remain difficult to experience until we come into a state of acceptance.

Conversely, we easily experience the emotions that we typically think of as positive because they occur during situations and events that we perceive as acceptable or even highly favorable. Such emotional energies move easily within a psychoenergetic matrix of openness, pleasure, and desire. Our easier emotions arise as continuing energetic support for favorable circumstances; such emotions remain easy to experience as long as we remain accepting.

Most emotions phase through periods of ease and difficulty as our perceptions of and responses to circumstances naturally change. Grief may start out as terribly difficult, heartwrenching pain; but if we effectively use its clearing and healing energies then grief slowly takes on a bittersweet quality, grows easier to feel, and may eventually become a profound healing presence. Pleasure typically arises as the easiest of feelings, yet a mere flicker of compulsiveness or abuse can turn things unpleasant in an instant. The ease or difficulty of any emotion depends on how fully we accept all aspects of our present situation, including the energy-in-motion.

Whether we ultimately use any emotion poorly or well depends on what we do with its energies. As waves of emotional energy move within, we take on greater power to respond to any given situation. The nature of our response—and we typically have a range of choices—determines how we use our vital energies. This in turn influences our circumstances, and as they shift so does our perception of those circumstances. This again changes the quantity and quality of emotional energy moving within, which empowers us to respond anew.

Ideally, emotional response becomes a fluid, ever-shifting process as we search for appropriate and effective ways to use our energies-in-motion. To the extent that we "go with the flow" of emotional energy—allowing its constant changing, yet taking full responsibility for its ultimate effects—we tend to use even the most difficult of emotions well. To the extent that we resist the flow of emotional energy—struggling with its constant changing and denying its ultimate effects—then we use even the easiest of emotions poorly.

When we work with emotional energy proactively, we tend to feel good about ourselves and our lives. When we refuse to work with, deny, and struggle against emotional energy, then we feel bad about ourselves and deal poorly with our lives.

Whether we ultimately feel good or not depends less on circumstances than on our chosen responses to the emotional energies aroused by circumstances.

For example, imagine waking on your wedding day to torrential rain. You have planned an outdoor wedding and you and your spouse-to-be felt so certain that you would get good weather that you decided not to "waste money" on a tent. The rain just keeps coming down. How could you not feel gloomy, depressed, frustrated, embarrassed, angry?

For some people such feelings become the final outcome: "It rained on our wedding day, and we both felt so mad at each other for not having a backup plan that we decided to postpone the wedding. We could never stop arguing about whose fault it was, and we eventually split up." For other people the difficult feelings provide energy for a flurry of creative thinking: "So then it occurred to us that the town movie theater is closed on Sundays, so we got the whole wedding party redirected, and we got married up on the stage with everyone filling the theater. They even came up with a cartoon in place of the wedding march."

We do not have negative emotions because bad things happen and positive emotions because good things happen. Rather, we naturally generate emotional energy in response to the varied changes of life; our overall experience of any emotion as positive or negative derives from personal choices and actions. We cause our immediate experience of any emotion to feel easy or difficult through our willingness to accept our perception of whatever happens. We cause the ultimate outcome of any movement of emotional energy through what we actually do with the energy. To a great extent, we cause life's unfolding circumstances through this never-ending process of feeling, experiencing, and using emotional energy.

—◀○▶—

Hushing Breath

Now, even as you read, bring attention to the movement of your breath.

Notice that you can read these words and make sense of their meaning,

While at the same time you can pay attention to the steady movement of your breath.

Now breathe in deeply through your nose, filling your torso,

And breathe out through the mouth in a long, soft, hushing sound, sssshhhh. . . .

Let the air go all the way out, without tensing, until you can no longer make the sound.

And then breathe in deeply through your nose, filling your torso,

And breathe out through the mouth in a long, soft, hushing sssshhhh. . . .

Make the sound until empty . . . and then breathe in again, filling your torso,

And breathe out through the mouth in a long, soft, hushing sssshhhh. . . .

Make the sound until empty . . . and then breathe in again, filling your torso,

And breathe out through the mouth in a long, soft, hushing sssshhhh. . . .

As you continue this breathing, let the movements of the breath become fluid and easy,

Breathing out until empty and without tensing or holding,

Breathing in until full and without tensing or holding,

One continuous, always gentle flowing breath. . . .

3

Emotional Suppression

Our conscious reasoning mind knows that negative feelings such as anger, fear, and regret are not wholly acceptable to ourselves or society, so it finds ways to suppress them, to push them into remote areas of our consciousness in order to forget them. Because we want to avoid suffering, we create defense mechanisms that deny the existence of these negative feelings and give us the impression we have peace within ourselves. But our internal formations are always looking for ways to manifest as destructive images, feelings, thoughts, words, or behavior.

—THICH NHAT HANH, *PEACE IS EVERY STEP*

An ideal life: Emotional energy flows throughout the body in regular, life-sustaining currents and extends beyond the body in radiant, life-connecting fields. You experience this always-moving energy as a quiet, gentle tingling (almost tickling) sensation and a systemwide feeling of simple pleasure. You feel good. This good feeling subsists as your ground of being—

the primary matrix through which you perceive, experience, and respond.

As life unfolds, the quantity and quality of your emotional energy ever changes, appropriate to the moment. The loss of a loved one arouses waves of sadness-energy, as surely as violations arouse anger-energy and threats arouse fear-energy. You accept the immediate movement of vital energy, respond well, use the energy, and then return to the simple tingling pleasure. All emotions come easily, and you spend their energies in a timely manner.

We search in vain for such lives. Even those who display the most emotional freedom and verve—artists, musicians, actors, and the like—experience more than their share of emotional dysfunction. Indeed, as we shall see, the odds of anyone reaching adulthood with a healthy, functioning emotional system approach zero.

We do, however, all come into the world with just such a system. Human life begins as infinitesimal mass emerging from near-infinite energy. The extraordinary growth that starts in the womb and continues through our early years results from a primordial energy-into-mass conversion process. From conception forward, our development as bodies, minds, and personalities depends on the vitality of our living energy and its free flow through all of our psychophysical systems.

Infants develop as flexible, malleable, fluid bodies suffused and enveloped with energy-in-motion. Any blocks or inhibitions of an infant's energy flow can cause developmental delay or disease. Healthy development depends on vital flowing energy, which means that healthy infants *feel* every waking moment.

The beatific smile of a gently born baby expresses peace as surely as the screaming of a just-circumcised baby expresses rage. Contrary to the notion that they have no emotions, babies experience perpetual emotion. Moreover, as with adults, this always-moving emotional energy serves as the empowering force for effective response to the constant flux of environment and events.

Obviously, babies do not have the wide range of emotional responses available to adults. Babies cannot express themselves verbally, cannot fight, cannot run away, and can do little to alter their environment or the people they encounter. While they surely experience threat, violation, and loss, babies have but two basic responses: they enjoy or they cry.

When babies emotionally respond with expressions of enjoyment—with their cuddles and coos, their trusting smiles, their beaming eyes, their grasping fingers, and their tasting mouths—they invoke feelings of love and nurturing from their parents and other caregivers. Enjoyment serves as the most creative of emotions: it can engender good caregiving and a supportive environment. Happy babies bond easily with the people in their world, who in turn respond with love and caring.

Yet many events in a baby's day will arouse difficult emotional energies. Hunger, wet diapers, teething and other physical pains, or being left alone: at such times the baby will experience strong waves of difficult emotional energy and will express that energy in the only way possible—through crying. For most babies, crying serves as an effective response: it gets a caregiver's attention and leads to the prompt alleviation of the problem.

Thus the natural emotional responses of the infant perfectly serve its current survival and ultimate development. Enjoyment cultivates bonding, love, and nurturance, while crying deals with immediate threats, losses, and violations. Moreover, when the adults do their part and respond appropriately, they condition infants to patterns of healthy emotional response.

In an ideal world this dance of emotional response between infants and adults would continue unabated through all the years of childhood development. Children would grow into adults with healthy, functioning emotional systems and would pass the lessons on to the next generation. All people would share an understanding of the essential purpose of emotional energy and would practice acceptance of emotional response in all of its forms.

In our not-so-ideal world, quite the contrary happens. Parents, teachers, and other adults struggle with children's expressions of emotional energy from birth onward. Because adults themselves have dysfunctional emotional systems, they pass emotional dysfunction on to their children. Because adults fail to appreciate the dynamics of emotional response, they deal poorly with much of their children's emotional expression.

Though the details differ from culture to culture and family to family, parents everywhere teach their children that they must suppress certain emotions. We condition children to accept some emotions but to deny others, to see some emotions as favorable and others as bad. We equate sadness with weakness, so we refuse to pick up our crying babies and we warn older children that "big boys and girls don't cry." We make clear that good girls and boys never express anger at their parents or teachers, however violated they may feel. We declare that being big and brave means showing no fear, no matter how frightening life becomes.

The lessons change from one child to another, but all children learn to sometimes deny some of their emotions. For too many children, the lessons come reinforced with the back of a hand or a verbal insult. The parent shouts, "Stop that crying this instant or I'll give you something to really cry about!" Or the parent spanks the child for expressing anger, until any expression of anger ceases. Or the parent ridicules and belittles the child for feeling afraid: "There's no such thing as monsters, now go to sleep!"

Even in the most loving of families adults tend to welcome and reward the child's easier emotions while denying and resisting the more difficult ones. We can hardly blame parents for preferring happy, smiling children over cranky, whining, screaming ones. As every parent knows too well, some situations compel us to do whatever it takes to STOP a child's emotional expression NOW (supermarket tantrums come to mind). Still, as well-intended and immediately necessary as such demands may seem, the child learns that some feelings cause trouble (bad boy!) and can lead to various unpleasant consequences, including the loss of love.

The child's easier emotions also come under attack. We may insist that our children rein in their boiling energies—that they slow down, that they cease their unending babble or at least talk a little softer, that they please stop singing that song over and over, that they go find something else to do and give Mommy and Daddy some peace and quiet. Again, at times even the best parents have little choice but to stifle their children.

Insisting that children control their emotional expression as a necessary aspect of maturity, however, means actively suppressing the pulsing, luminous promise of childhood. Unfortunately, the more adults struggle with their own emotional energies, the more they will struggle with the naturally bursting exuberance of children and the more they will demand, "Rein it in, control it, stop it."

Grow up. Now. Or else.

And so, because children will do whatever they must to survive, and because children want love and acceptance more than anything else, they learn to suppress—to rein in, to control, to stop—the essential energies of emotional response.

Suppression means "to press down." When we suppress an emotion we actively force the energy-in-motion down into ourselves; we stanch, stifle, or restrict its flow. Rather than move through us to manifest in some form of response, the emotional energy contracts within, loses vigor, and expresses weakly, if at all.

Any act of suppression involves three elements. First, suppression always begins with an attitude of disapproval and refusal. For reasons that seem compelling in the moment, we say no to our immediate experience, including our feelings.

For example, an infant may be left alone to cry itself to sleep at night, with the parents thinking it will cultivate strength and independence in their child (while getting some much-needed peace for themselves). The simultaneous experience of loss, violation, and threat naturally arouses strong emotional energy for the child, which expresses through crying. But in this case the crying fails to resolve the problem. Nobody comes to the child's aid and the aloneness persists. Further, the unabated crying feels terrible. After a time, the child will reject the whole affair—the experience of "alone in the dark" and the emotions aroused—by resisting and refusing the present movement of life-energy.

The child says no to his or her immediate experience and takes a critical step in learning to suppress emotional energy— holding it in rather than crying it out. This may actually help the child to sleep, since the work of suppressing strong emotional energy causes fatigue. However, such experiences typically generalize toward future behavior; the child initiates a pattern of emotional suppression, which will show up in similar circumstances and may persist throughout life.

Conditioned by their parents and other caregivers, all children come to reject— to say no to—certain emotions. Because crying failed to help in the past, the child resists feeling sad in the present. Because expressions of anger have caused violent parental reactions, the child thinks, "I must never get angry." Because the grown-ups keep insisting, "There's nothing to be afraid of," the child learns to hate feeling afraid.

With maturity our ways of saying no to emotion become more complex and finely reasoned. Men come to equate sadness with girlishness and strive to avoid it at all costs. Women come to see expressions of anger as shrill, strident, and unladylike. Fear becomes evidence of immaturity, or of weakness, irrationality, or lack of spirit. We denounce overexhuberance as uncool, and we try not to laugh too hard or care too much. We struggle with feelings of pleasure and sexual arousal that occur at inappropriate times and places.

At the root of all such attitudes resides a thought: I do not want this feeling. I reject, resist, and refuse it. I choose *not* to accept this moment's energy-in-motion.

I do not want to feel: the first element of emotional suppression.

The second element involves some degree of physical tension. To stifle the flow of emotional energy we must physically contract and tighten some part or parts of the body. This can mean the whole body, as when a person becomes paralyzed with fear. More often we tighten specific parts of the body: the clenched jaw and fists of anger, the caved-in chest and slumping shoulders of sadness, the furrowed brow of worry, the down-turned lips of a frown, the tired eyes and blurred vision of overwhelming stress.

Emotional energy normally flows through the softer tissues of the physical body—the muscles, tendons, skin, and fascia. When we do not want to feel an emotion we instinctively contract those areas of the body; we narrow and constrict the very medium through which the emotional energy would move. We physically suppress emotion by physically contracting the channels of energy-in-motion.

As emotional suppression becomes habitual and automatic, so does physical tension in the midst of emotional experience. So whenever we feel sad our chest becomes heavy. Whenever we feel angry we grind our teeth. Whenever we feel anxious we clench our toes. Whenever we feel anything that we would rather not feel some part of our bodies instinctively contracts as we unconsciously attempt to control the feeling, to rein it in, to stifle it. With time we come to equate the physical stress of emotional suppression with emotion itself, an unfortunate misunderstanding that only reinforces the first element of emotional suppression: of course we do not want to feel, since feeling involves such pain and tension.

The mind says no to the energy-in-motion. The body contracts and obstructs the natural pathways of the energy.

The third element of emotional suppression involves our breathing. In order to suppress any emotion, we must actively suppress the breath. We constrict the flow of breath in any of several ways: by tightening the throat, sealing the lips, sinking the chest, freezing the belly, and stiffening the neck and shoulders. Or we control the pace and rhythm of the breath: by breathing slower or more shallowly, or by unconsciously holding the breath in or out.

We can easily observe the suppression of breath in others and ourselves. Watch a young child trying hard not to cry: sealed, quivering lips, sunken chest, slumping shoulders, and barely perceptible breathing. Watch somebody controlling strong anger: clenched jaw; stiffened muscles throughout the upper torso, neck, and face; and tightly held breath. Notice the lack of breath in a doctor's waiting room, during a critical test in school, or in the closing moments of a tense sporting event. Observe your own breathing when asking the boss for a raise, getting criticized by someone in authority, worrying about money, or trying hard not to laugh at an inappropriate moment.

Whenever we do not want to feel we instinctively and unconsciously breathe less.

The breath occupies a special place in the human experience. As a function of the respiratory system it has an obvious physical dimension, and constricting the breath always involves the physical tensing of various body parts. Breath also has a mental dimension; our thoughts, attitudes, and beliefs affect our breathing, while every breath directly affects our mental experience. The breath also relates closely to the vital energies that flow within and around humans; flowing breath, flowing energy, and flowing emotions share common origins and patterns of movement.

In practice, our efforts to understand and work with emotional energy and to overcome suppression compel us to think holistically—to see body, mind, spirit, and emotions as one interrelated system. The three elements of emotional suppression arise simultaneously rather than sequentially. We cannot separate the mental rejection of a feeling from the physical stifling of that feeling and the immediate suppression of breath. Each connects synergistically to the other, and we successfully suppress emotional energy only by doing all three. Conversely, by *undoing* any of these three elements we can avoid emotional suppression in the present and begin to heal from the effects of suppression in the past.

◄○►

Belly Breath

Now, even as you read, bring attention to the movement of your breath.

Breathe in deeply through your nose, filling your torso,

And breathe out through the mouth in a long, soft, hushing sound, sssshhhh. . . .

Let the air go all the way out, without tensing, until you can no longer make the sound,

And then breathe in deeply through your nose, filling your torso,

And breathe out through the mouth in a long, soft, hushing sssshhhh. . . .

Now, as you continue this breathing, pay attention to the movements of your lower belly.

As you breathe in, allow your belly to expand,

Becoming full and round with vital energy.

As you breathe out, your belly empties and flattens, sssshhhh. . . .

Every breath in, your belly expands; every breath out, your belly empties, sssshhhh. . . .

Continue this breathing, these deep, gentle breaths,

Your belly rhythmically expanding and emptying, even as you read. . . .

4

The Costs of
Suppression

*The world of feeling is unpredictable, confusing, and
hard to control. That is the nature of feeling. . . . Some
people are fortunate enough to grow up in families
that teach that it is all right to experience feelings
and tell the truth about them. Many families—perhaps
most—teach their children strategies that become
problems for us later.*

—Gay and Kathlyn Hendricks, *At the Speed of Life*

Emotional suppression sometimes serves a useful, even essential purpose. When suffering a severe traumatic injury the
body automatically passes into the physiological state of
shock, blocking all feeling and sensation and numbing consciousness, so that the injured person can better begin recov-
ery. Similarly, when children experience physical, emotional,
or sexual abuse, they commonly report feeling numb, los-
ing consciousness, and sometimes even leaving their bodies

(they may remember objectively observing the event from above). In such cases emotional suppression serves as a mercy, a blessing, and a necessary first step in the healing process.

Even during lesser travails suppression often seems the best we can do. As children learn early on, no matter how much a parent (or boss, policeman, or other authority figure) may violate you, it rarely helps to vent your rage. Indeed, expressing anger-energy typically makes matters worse. Grief-stricken as you may feel, crying does not always help—especially around other people who will not abide tears, or when the time and energy given to crying might interfere with something else that needs to get done. The same goes with fear: showing your fear to others can undermine your ability to lead or interfere with the need for immediate action. Some situations seem to offer no other choice than to suppress a feeling now, such as needing to laugh during a funeral or experiencing sexual arousal at the wrong time or place or around the wrong person.

We mostly suppress emotions as a way to avoid expressing them. All social groups, beginning with the family, develop their own sets of good manners and mores, which govern the acceptable and unacceptable times for emotional expression. A society full of people all spontaneously expressing their emotions threatens unending chaos. In order to form polite, civil, working groups, individuals must somehow control their emotional energies; maturing socially means learning to rein in our natural (but childish) tendency for emotional expression.

Yet while emotional suppression may sometimes serve a useful purpose, inhibiting the free flow of emotional energies over the course of a lifetime causes serious damage to our bodies, minds, and spirits. Our efforts to stifle emotion become a stifling of life itself. Though the symptoms vary, most people die from a slow suicide of self-strangulation. Therefore it behooves us to understand just how badly emotional suppression injures us, even as we find healthier ways to deal with ever-flowing emotional energies.

Emotional suppression causes systemwide dysfunction and disease.

When we suppress an emotion, the energy of that emotion does not go away. Instead, it subsides—it sinks deeper. Rather than resolve the emotional energy through some form of response, we choose (however unconsciously) to hold it inside. Though the immediacy of the feeling may pass, the energy does not. We hold it deep inside and, typically, it stays inside.

Modern physics tells us that mass becomes energy as energy becomes mass. Though emotional energy forms the most subtle stuff, it *is* stuff nonetheless. If you hold enough of this stuff inside you, then you become energetically "stuffed up," which carries the same implications as a stuffed nose, stuffed colon, stuffed arteries, or even owning too much stuff.

Energy moves within the body in regular currents and beyond the body in radiant fields. As emotional suppression becomes an unconscious habit and emotional energy becomes stuffed inside, the free movement of vital energy gradually degrades. Think of a wide rushing river into which one daily throws several large stones. Over the course of a lifetime the river becomes clogged, diminished, and sluggish. Likewise, over the course of a human lifetime the habitual suppression of emotional energy clogs and diminishes the once-rushing river of light.

As we clog and diminish the flow of emotional energy we block and interfere with the fundamental design and function of the human organism. This causes systemwide dysfunction, with most biological processes and organs (including the brain/mind) failing to operate at full efficiency. Life spans shorten and creative potential declines. Sickness, disease, and general unhappiness all take a larger-than-necessary role in the human drama. Our bodies and minds struggle through energy-starved lives, while suppressing great wells of life force within.

Emotional suppression inflicts specific injuries upon the body.

This occurs when, especially as children, we must suppress extremely traumatic emotions. The child who has just suffered a severe violation or who has suddenly learned of a huge loss will experience a great burst of emotional energy in response. If for immediately compelling reasons the child suppresses that emotion, then all of the child's surging energy becomes forcefully jammed *somewhere in particular* in the body.

The specific location will relate in some way to the specifics of the situation. If the child suffers physical injury, then emotional suppression may occur at the site of the injury. If the child contracts into a grimace or a frown, then emotional energy may lock in the muscles of the face. Anywhere that the child experiences pain or tension during the traumatic event—clenched fists, upset stomach, spanked bottom, abused genitals—becomes a likely place to harbor suppressed emotional energies. And unless the child later experiences deep healing the suppressed energies of a traumatic event remain embodied forever.

When a strong charge of vital energy contracts in the body for a long period of time, the energy eventually becomes matter. The energy literally becomes an unhealthy, pathological mass. Suppressed emotional energy can become tumorous, harden arteries, stiffen joints, weaken bones. Suppressed emotional energy can precipitate the onset of cancer in any system or organ of the body. Suppressed emotional energy can undermine the immune system and make a body vulnerable to innumerable illnesses.

Ironically, what begins as a gift of vital energy and the raw material for empowered response turns into its opposite: the stuff of dysfunction and disease. The choice to contract and suppress traumatic emotional energy plants energy-charged seeds of future pathology. The more urgently a child suppresses a traumatic event, or the more often the child experiences a less traumatic event (such as a specific criticism that a child hears several times a day, every day, over a period of years), the more potentially destructive the specific quantity of suppressed energy.

The typical adult body, as any experienced bodyworker will tell you, comes riddled with the suppressed emotional energies of the past. Bodywork is a growing field of alternative medicine whose modalities include various forms and combinations of movement, sound, breath, and physical manipulation. The latter ranges from the gentle touching to often painful probing of deep tissues. Often the simplest of touches to some innocuous part of the body, when expertly applied, will release a torrent of emotion and long-suppressed memory. The powerful healing that such work can initiate testifies to the destructive effects of long-term emotional suppression.

Emotional suppression renders us less capable and responsible.

Ideally, energy-in-motion empowers us to deal more effectively with the changes and challenges of life. Through the unconscious habit of suppressing emotional energy, however, we misplace the very essence of effective response. The person who habitually suppresses all feelings of fear will stand frozen in the road unable to leap out of the way of approaching traffic. The person who suppresses all feelings of sadness will fail to fully resolve painful losses and may always suffer from low-grade chronic grief. The person who habitually suppresses anger will feel forever cowed and victimized by the inevitable violations of life. The person who suppresses feelings of sexual pleasure will derive little satisfaction from lovemaking and may manifest various forms of sexual aberration.

We need our emotions. They provide us with the vital force to think creatively and act decisively. The more successfully we suppress our emotions, the less successfully we do anything else.

Emotional suppression deforms the body.

Whenever we suppress an emotion we physically contract some part or parts of the body. In time we develop patterns of repeated emotional suppression, which means that specific parts of the body must engage in chronic tension. Such long-term chronic tension eventually alters body form and posture, invariably for the worse.

The "character lines" etched into an older person's face result from years of tensing the face while struggling with emotional energy. A permanently hunched upper back reveals a person who never made peace with burdens and responsibilities, just as a caved-in chest shows us someone overwhelmed with unresolved grief. Years of fearing and resisting sex can tilt the pelvis back and away from other people. Angrily clenching the jaw will eventually grind the enamel off of teeth, just as chronically clenching toes will shorten tendons in the feet, with ramifications throughout the body.

Bodyworkers have cataloged many such examples of emotional suppression leading to misshapen bodies. The tree will grow as we bend the twig. As human bodies grow, incalculable bending comes from the chronic physical contraction of emotional suppression.

Emotional suppression causes systemwide fatigue.

Suppressing strong emotion does not occur easily. It requires an act of forceful muscular contraction, stifled breath, and mental denial to engineer the original suppression of an emotion—the stronger the emotion, the more force required—and it requires continuing contraction and denial to sustain such suppression. Without the expenditure of great quantities of energy, emotional suppression could not and would not occur. Typically, as a person ages more and more emotional energy becomes suppressed, while more and more vital energy is tied up in sustaining suppression. All of which just plain wears us down.

Emotional suppression undermines the healthy function of body and mind and stuffs inside the rushing energy of effective response. To make matters worse, emotional suppression requires that we permanently commit significant amounts of energy to keeping everything stuffed away, unfelt and unnoticed. This places heavy demands on our daily resources. So much of the chronic fatigue that afflicts people in modern societies stems from this unconscious sustaining of emotional suppression. Though we have access to great wells of vital energy, we can only lose so much to the dynamics of suppression before we become chronically enervated.

Emotional suppression energetically disconnects us from the rest of our world.

The energy fields that surround a healthy human being extend outward to touch and meaningfully connect with other people and the environment. Through these vital energy connections we experience oneness and can communicate with others in the most profound and satisfying ways. Positive emotions, such as love, compassion, empathy, intimacy, and trust, only occur between people who can connect energetically. Telepathy works in the same way; we experience better nonverbal communication with those with whom we have the greatest intimacy simply because we have more energy links through which to transfer information.

The more we expand our energy-selves, the healthier our relationships become. Conversely, the more we suppress our emotions the less we can energy-connect with others and the more difficulty we have with basic human relationship. A tight and chronically suppressed person has contracted his or her energy fields in and away from others and becomes effectively disconnected and less able to relate.

All forms of communication seem difficult for the "energy-disabled." When we have the sense that another person "just doesn't get it," it indicates some degree of energetic contraction and disconnection we have from one another. The most sincere efforts at verbal communication quite literally go nowhere once we have severed our energy links. Even worse, we sever our innate capacities for *feeling* other people. We cannot experience empathy, compassion, trust, or love without the genuine oneness engendered by vital emotional-energetic connection.

Such disconnection takes an enormous toll. The worst of human behavior occurs between those who become energy-disconnected. All of our violence, wars and oppressions, racism and sexism, and various domination-driven inhumanities—such foolishness can only be perpetrated by those who have cut themselves off from "the other." We cannot intentionally hurt another person (or animal, plant, or ecosystem) with whom we experience living oneness. To the contrary, before we actively attack or exploit another person or group we must first sever our common links. Before we lash out, we must first suppress, contract, disconnect, and separate.

Our modern world teems with men and women who have been conditioned to emotional suppression since early childhood. They stumble through and struggle with the unceasing waves of emotional experience that define any life. They hide from grief and run from fear and collapse in the face of anger. They seem perplexed by the simplest pleasures. They suppress their emotions defensively, reflexively, unconsciously. Much of their natural biological and intellectual potential has become dammed up, rendering them more vulnerable to disease and dysfunction and less capable of dealing with the challenges of human existence. They lack the boiling-over enthusiasm for life that they knew as children; they instead feel chronically fatigued, tired all the time.

These unfortunate emotional cripples treat one another abysmally. How could they not? They have had the essence of their humanity conditioned out of them, and they routinely submit their children to the same conditioning. They have become incapable of feeling—simply feeling—the insanity of it all.

◀◯▶

Tension Release Breath

Now, even as you read, bring attention to the movement of your breath.

Now breathe in slowly through the nose and, as you inhale,

Tightly clench your toes, tightly clench your hands, and tightly clench your jaw.

Continue to slowly inhale while creating tension in your feet, hands, and jaw.

And now release that tension with a long, soft, gentle sssshhhh. . . .

Again, breathe in slowly through the nose and, as you inhale,

Tightly clench your toes, your hands, and your jaw,

Creating as much tension as possible in your feet, hands, and jaw.

And now release that tension with a long, soft, gentle sssshhhh. . . .

Once more, breathe in slowly through the nose and, as you inhale,

Tightly clench your toes, your hands, and your jaw,

Creating as much tension as possible in your feet, hands, and jaw.

And now release that tension with a long, soft, gentle sssshhhh. . . .

Now pay attention to the movements of your lower belly.

As you breathe in, allow your belly to expand,

Becoming full and round with vital energy.

As you breathe out, your belly empties and flattens, sssshhhh. . . .

Every breath in, your belly expands, every breath out, your belly empties.

Continue this breathing, these deep, gentle breaths,

Your belly rhythmically expanding and emptying, even as you read. . . .

5

Flow

If your every day practice is to open to all your emotions, to all the people you meet, to all the situations you encounter, without closing down, trusting that you can do that—then that will take you as far as you can go.

And then you'll understand all the teachings that anyone has ever taught.

—PEMA CHÖDRON, *WHEN THINGS FALL APART*

When we think of emotion we usually have in mind the active and outward expression of emotional energy. We equate sadness with crying, anger with ranting, fear with trembling, happiness with smiling, joy with laughing. We consider such external manifestations of emotional energy as the emotions themselves. We call the person "emotional" who allows the visible or auditory display, or *expression*, of emotional energy.

As a way to experience emotion expression avoids most of the life-threatening, long-term consequences of suppression.

Our bodies especially fare better when we vent the energy of strong emotion outward rather than contract and hold it inside. The person who cries easily and often exhibits better health in the long run than the person who cannot cry at all, as does the person who spontaneously expresses anger when it arises (though out-of-control bursts of anger carry their own risks of hurting people and breaking things).

Yet expression generally fails to address the germinal cause of specific emotional energy. Some people cry for years and years without ever getting over their losses, just as others rage on and on without ever resolving their anger. Blowing off steam keeps the teakettle from exploding but does nothing to alter the source of the heat or prevent the generation of more steam. Likewise, expression avoids many of the problems of suppression but nonetheless results in a failed and frustrating emotional experience.

Expression frustrates. From the first time that crying fails to bring a competent, loving caregiver, through a lifetime of misfired rants and embarrassing gaffes, the continued expression of emotional energy leaves a history of confusion, disappointment, and shame. Expression rarely works—it rarely brings about the successful resolution of an event—and its near certain promise of frustration becomes a primary cause of chronic suppression.

In practice, failed emotional expression involves the same three elements as emotional suppression. The man who holds the attitude that crying in front of others means weakness will create tension in various parts of the body while sobbing, will struggle with choppy, halting breath, and will later feel shame or embarrassment rather than resolution. The woman who attempts to vent her rage through a body chronically racked with physical tension and choked breath will never find satisfaction, no matter how hard she tries. The same applies to any other emotional expression: when it comes with any combination of an unaccepting attitude, physical tension, and stifled breathing, then what caused the emotion remains unresolved and emotional frustration results.

It seems we have only two choices when experiencing emotion—either we express emotional energy outward or we suppress the energy inward—and each choice has its own drawbacks. However, although suppression plants the seeds of long-term negative consequences, the short-term consequences of expression seem much worse. Suppression goes on below the surface; expression happens visibly, audibly, dramatically. We pass our days largely unaware of the dangers of suppression, while expression can cause immediate and all too obvious difficulties. It should therefore not surprise us that suppression becomes the predominant way of dealing with emotions in most families and societies.

Adults condition children mostly toward suppression. Simply imagine the utter chaos of children everywhere expressing all their emotions all the time. In order to form peaceful, orderly, and productive unions, most social groups, beginning with the family, determine the need to limit emotional expression among all members, beginning with children.

Yet people never stop having emotions. We cannot prevent the arousal of emotional energy in response to specific events any more than we can prevent breathing or thinking. Since both expression and suppression more or less frustrate the original purpose of aroused emotional energy, we rarely experience the successful resolution of an emotion, nor of the event that generated the emotional energy. All of which, again, only feeds into prevailing patterns of suppressing and denying most emotions.

Fortunately, we do have another choice with emotional energy: we can move beyond our patterns of emotional expression and suppression as we allow, go with, enhance, and expand the experience of *flow*.

Flow describes a naturally occurring state of consciousness during which emotions work—they fulfill their purpose by providing the energy needed to successfully respond to circumstances and events. When you perceive a threat to your well-being and feel an immediate rush of strong fear-energy that propels you toward decisive action, then you have experienced the state of flow. The same is true when you learn of the death of a loved one and feel an immediate swell of sadness-energy that moves you through the stages of grief in a timely manner, or when you perceive a serious violation and feel an immediate surge of anger-energy that empowers you to emphatically deal with the violator.

Flow integrates all aspects of a human being. Flow occurs when our disparate and divided self comes together and functions as a whole. The experience of flow allows work to seem effortless, creativity to come easily, and relationships to find their natural harmony. In flow we describe ourselves as "in a groove," "on a roll," "in the zone," "on top of our game," "in synch." We feel unbeatable, unstoppable, and in control.

Unlike suppression, which pathologically stuffs energy-in-motion inside, flow fully accepts and decisively uses emotional energy. Unlike expression, which threatens recklessness and loss of control, flow brings an acute awareness of the current situation and of one's creative role within unfolding events.

Every emotion has both an inward and outward dimension. During expression, emotional energy comes streaming out of a person in audible and visible display, while mind, body, breath, and energy contract within. During suppression, the energy becomes contracted both within and without. In the case of flow, emotional energy moves within the body as a strong and vital force yet may or may not show any trace of external manifestation.

The internal movement of emotional energy or lack thereof ultimately determines whether an emotion frustratingly expresses, pathologically suppresses, or effectively flows. Once we contract the inward-flowing energy-in-motion, it matters little whether we express some of the energetic content of the emotion or we suppress all release of energy; when we stifle the internal movement of energy, we lose the state of flow and consign ourselves to an experience of poorly used emotion and a less-than-favorable outcome of events.

The three elements of emotional suppression and frustrated expression—an unaccepting attitude, bodily tension, and stifled breath—cause the inward contraction of one's life-energy. Conversely, the same three elements reversed allow for and encourage the experience of emotional flow.

The first element of emotional flow involves an abiding attitude of *active acceptance*. Active acceptance means saying yes to present circumstances as fully and wholeheartedly as possible. One accepts whatever happens, including other people, the changing environment, the weather, one's body, one's thoughts, and especially the immediate energy-in-motion.

Note that such acceptance does not necessarily entail enjoying or desiring or agreeing with whatever happens. We can dislike, even dread, some situation while at the same time allowing that it occurs. Active acceptance means that we do not commit our energy to resisting, denying, or struggling against unfolding events. We accept life as it happens. Yet even as we feel accepting of our immediate experience, we can still desire and work for change.

Human biography has recorded many examples of people who have practiced active acceptance and thereby learned to flow, in the midst of horrible circumstances. From ex-prisoners, holocaust survivors, explorers, war veterans, and those who have recovered from catastrophic illness we can glean a recurring account of people who manage to not merely survive but thrive during their ordeals. Through all such stories runs a common thread of active acceptance; while not liking their circumstances, these people nonetheless take life as it comes and find ways to consciously and creatively engage in the present moment. In so doing they find some measure of active participation in events. They become creators rather than victims, and when their ordeals end and they return to their everyday worlds their creativity continues to blossom.

Conversely, those who simply will not accept unfolding events typically feel psychically and emotionally defeated by their experiences, even when they physically survive. The strongly held attitude of unacceptance destroys people from within, more surely than the worst of external circumstances. Whatever life brings, the practice of active acceptance ensures the most creative and potentially satisfying of responses.

Imagine riding in a canoe in turbulent, rushing waters. You must fully accept your place in the canoe, the canoe's place in the water, and the direction and speed of both the water and the canoe. Wishing to be somewhere else, to do something else, or to go in the opposite direction causes unproductive stress and difficulty. Instead you strive to go with the flow, and the better you flow, the better the outcome.

At the same time you should also have a paddle in your hands. The paddle enables you to use intent within the flow and choose your direction. Without a paddle, going with the flow could take you into shallow waters or crash you against rocks or send you over a waterfall. With a paddle you can actively and creatively exercise some measure of control over unfolding events.

As riders in the canoe of life it behooves us to fully surrender to whatever happens—to go with the flow—while simultaneously finding ways to responsibly influence perception and outcome. To practice surrender alone leaves us passive observers and likely victims of events, while overcontrolling at the expense of acceptance wastes energy and causes unnecessary struggle. Active acceptance requires that we integrate the seeming opposites of surrender and control. As we succeed in this emotional alchemy, we greatly enhance our experience of flow and the possibilities for the successful resolution of whatever happens.

The second element of emotional flow involves the *dynamic relaxation* of the body. During suppression and expression we create tension in various parts of the body in order to stifle our energy-in-motion. Over the course of a lifetime these physical tensions become chronic and more or less disabling. Flow occurs as we release such tensions while practicing and encouraging the experience of dynamic relaxation.

As massage therapists, acupuncturists, yoga teachers, and meditators have long known, and as medical studies have begun to substantiate, deep relaxation reduces harmful stress, encourages physical and emotional healing, clarifies the mind, and improves performance in many areas of life. Ten minutes a day of relaxation practice has been shown to have profound rejuvenating and transformational effects.

Dynamic relaxation differs from less effective forms of relaxation that we may achieve from the use of pharmaceuticals or alcohol, from watching television, or from the mere cessation of stressful circumstances (as when we take a vacation from a high-stress job). While such experiences certainly may relieve our tension, they do so by depressing the movement of vital energies. This slows us down but also clouds the brain and hampers present-time awareness. We feel enervated rather than alive. We become couch potatoes or beach blobs. Though such enervation may seem a necessary relief from the grinding stress of the everyday world, it comes without the deep healing benefits of dynamic relaxation and at the expense of our physical and emotional well-being.

The experience of dynamic relaxation combines a loose and rested body with a clear and focused mind. As any experienced athlete knows, the key to success lies in being totally awake and focused on the task at hand, while simultaneously keeping the body loose and free of tension. During any practice of dynamic relaxation energy flows easily through all systems to promote health, vitality, and inspired creation. Consequently, we flow more easily in general through varied circumstances and events.

We can achieve dynamic relaxation in any number of ways, ranging from deep meditation to mentally stimulating forms of hard work or exercise, or through the regular practice of yoga or tai chi, or by receiving massage and other forms of bodywork, or through the experience of good, loving sex. The best methods feel enjoyable when practiced and fit easily into our daily lives. Any effective method of deep relaxation will include an attitude of active acceptance, as well as the third element of emotional flow: *connected breathing.*

Connected breathing occurs when the inhale and exhale become continuous, one flowing into the other without interruption or pause. We may also use the terms *circular breathing,* suggesting breath that, like a circle, has neither beginning nor end; or *ocean breathing,* suggesting breath that becomes like the eternal inward and outward movement of ocean waves. In each case, we emphasize an ever-moving cycle of breath: always flowing in or flowing out, with as little stopping, holding, or contracting as possible.

We can witness this simple connected breathing in most

newborn babies, as well as in animals, including our pet cats and dogs, for those who have not struggled to suppress their emotional energies still breathe according to the body's innate design. A baby's breathing moves continuously, stopping only to deal with food, fluids, and gas. This connected breathing promotes the strong energy flow crucial to the extraordinary growth that babies undergo.

Just as the heart serves as the central mechanism of the circulatory system, so the breath serves as the central mechanism of our vital energy system. Interrupting the flow of breath makes no more sense—for the health of body and mind—than interrupting the beating of the heart.

Yet we learn to do precisely that. Early in life we find that some of our emotions greatly displease our parents and other caregivers, and we discover, albeit unconsciously, that we can stop the outward expression of an emotion, and much of its internal sensation, by contracting our breathing. Once we learn to stifle unwanted emotions by stifling breath, we undermine the body's "original breath" and develop in its place habits of unhealthy and dysfunctional breathing. Instead of supporting us our breathing turns chronically pathological; we habitually breathe in ways that suppress energy flow, with all of the negative consequences that suppression brings.

Yet the breath that suppresses us can also set us free. Conscious connected breathing offers the most direct way to vital and satisfying emotional flow. However difficult we may find it to fully accept our current circumstances, however racked with chronic tensions our bodies have become, we can *always* consciously sustain a gentle, flowing pattern of breath. Truly, it requires no more than that we bring awareness to our breathing and choose to let it flow in and then flow out. As our breathing flows we naturally find ourselves more accepting, more relaxed, and more easily flowing with all that happens.

◄O►

Energy Circle Breath

Now, even as you read, bring attention to the movement of your breath.

Now breathe in deeply through your nose, filling your torso,

And breathe out through the mouth in a long, soft, gentle sssshhhh. . . .

Again, breathe in deeply through your nose, filling your torso,

And breathe out through the mouth in a long, soft, gentle sssshhhh. . . .

Now, continuing with this breathing, feel or sense or imagine that as you inhale

Energy flows like a waterfall over your forehead and down your face, your throat,

Your chest, and down into your belly and genitals, filling, like water in a pool. . . .

Feel or sense or imagine that as you exhale, sssshhhh, the energy rushes up the spine,

Like a bursting fountain, up the spine to the top of the head, where, as you inhale,

It again flows like a waterfall down toward the belly and genitals.

Continue this slow, gentle breathing, every inhale flowing down the front of the body,

Filling the belly and genitals . . .

Every exhale rushing up the spine, like a fountain, to the top of the head. . . .

One continuous flowing breath,

One continuous circle of life-sustaining energy. . . .

6

Love

Why must we have a passion for reality? Why must we love and desire and be filled with metaphysical ardor? Because these passions set up in us the momentum for bringing new forms into being.

—JEAN HOUSTON, *THE POSSIBLE HUMAN*

We live in the age of connection. Through the wizardry of personal computers and the Internet we can come into instant, even intimate contact with others throughout the world, as well as with a huge and growing body of information. Satellites send pictures of distant planets back to Earth through light years of empty space, while cellular communication devices now allow us to link up at all times, in most places. From an early age we take for granted the invisible connections used by such wireless gadgets as portable radios, telephones, and remote controls.

This technology-based experience of connectedness finds confirmation in many of the life sciences. Holistic medicine asserts that all parts of the body interconnect and function as a single system; a change in any one part affects all other parts. Quantum physicists have demonstrated that invisible links exist between any two particles of matter, however great their seeming separation. Similar insights echo in the disciplines of environmental science, systems theory, computer programming, and global economics.

Everything connects. We live in a worldwide web, truly, as every living thing connects to every living thing.

Yet when it comes to a typical relationship between two or more people, or two or more groups of people, disconnection seems the prevailing truth. We live as if the body forms an impermeable boundary, dividing each of us from the rest of the world. We experience the self as inside the body and everything and everybody else as outside. At times, we open up and reach through the body-boundary to genuinely connect with some other. Mostly we remain separate and apart from others and, through various forms of intolerant thought, we justify, enforce, and even celebrate our disconnection.

Part of the problem stems from an inability to explain or even imagine a medium of connection between people. Our technological connectors all depend on one form or another of energy. Pull the plug, take out the battery, sever the wiring, or shut down the power plant and our computers, phones, satellites, televisions, radios, and remote control devices immediately stop working, their connections broken. Energy functions as the one essential force of technological connection.

Any such medium of connection between people, however, has proven difficult to scientifically verify. For many the very notion of invisible forces constitutes an insurmountable problem. Despite the model that our technologies provide—vast quantities of data flashing instantly and invisibly around the globe—the suggestion that similar connections exist between humans—enabling similar transfers of information—smacks of quackery and long-discredited vitalism.

For others, God presents just such an invisible, omniscient, and omnipresent (if ultimately unfathomable and scientifically unverifiable) force that connects all people. Yet God obviously means different things to different people and, for too many, God remains abstract, distant and apart from humanity. Defined and experienced as such, God not only fails to serve as a medium of connection, He, She, or It actually becomes a justification for decidedly disconnected behavior, as our long history of religion-based wars and intolerance demonstrates.

Still, many cultures have long had experience with an invisible force that connects humans. They have given it many names—including num, chi, prana, mana, animal magnetism, life-energy, and the soul's substance—and they all describe a similar vibratory force that moves through the body in regular currents and emanates beyond the body in radiant fields. As we have seen, allowing this energy to flow more freely through the body brings great benefits to our physical health and general well-being. Now we will explore the positive implications of the fields of energy that extend beyond our bodies.

Just as energy moves within us as the motive force and raw material for effective response to life's constant changing, so energy extends beyond the body in radiant fields (called *auras*) that connect us to the world, or to specific others, and that vary in size, intensity, and feeling according to our ever-changing perceptions and intentions. For a strong and healthy individual and for most babies, the energy fields extend vigorously from the body, filling entire rooms and beyond, while providing vital links to the living world. The energy "boils over," as the Kung would say, and flows out into meaningful connection with our world. The larger and more vital our energy fields, the more energy-connected we feel, and the more empowered we become to meet life's challenges.

These fields all grow out of and expand from in-flowing energy-in-motion. Thus, the more vigorously we flow within, the larger and more vital our radiant fields. Yet while we may experience our internal energy-in-motion as positive one moment and negative the next, we mostly feel our out flowing energy as a positive (though not always easy) force. As a rule, the expansion of our vital energy occurs as a positive, life-affirming, and uplifting event.

Exceptions to this rule do exist. Powerful and out-of-control desires, such as lust and greed, will send waves of clutching energy toward the object of desire. Extreme hatred and anger can explode outward in malevolent waves. Disciplined practitioners of the "black arts" can learn to extend their energy fields with purely evil intent. Certain political and religious leaders, such as Adolf Hitler or Jim Jones, have used their charisma—their "personal magnetism"—to manipulate large numbers of followers with energy-based mass influence.

Yet such negative expansions of life force tend toward self-depletion and self-destruction. Like plants growing from poisoned soil, vital energy radiating from a toxic, chronically suppressed being will poison all that it touches, beginning with the mind and body of the offending individual. Clearly, such people can inflict great suffering in the world with their psychoenergetic powers. But they practice a form of self-immolation as they must ever dwell within and eventually choke on their own toxic radiation.

While any negative expansions of vital energy invariably bring us to self-deplete and self-destruct, positive expansions of energy bring the very opposite results: they make us stronger, healthier, more energized and alive. Curiosity, for instance, sends energy tendrils out to ask and inquire of things, to touch and taste the world; the more curious we feel, the more we learn, and the greater our curiosity becomes. The protective concern that parents feel for their children extends like strong energy arms that—despite the countless worries children inspire—never grow tired of reaching to surround and protect. Deeply heartfelt dreams start waves of energy pulsing through manifest reality; the more committed our dream, the more our dream-energy expands, and the more likely our chances of successful creation.

Any positive expansion of vital energy has the potential to sustain itself indefinitely, while sustaining the self at the most basic levels. When we expand our energy with positive intent we step into an infinite river of living spirit. The more we give outward, the more energy arises within and the more empowered we become to go on giving. No experience demonstrates this better than love.

Love emanates from within as moving and outward expanding energy. When we love any other—person, animal, plant, place, or thing—we extend our self, as fields of living energy, to touch, to envelop, to enter into, to couple with the other. We feel the outward-connecting movement of our energy as love.

Love enhances flow, so when we love we reap precious blessings for ourselves. Our bodies function better on all levels. Our natural healing processes can accelerate, causing the spontaneous remission of the most difficult of diseases. Love-inspired minds become clearer, lighter, and positively directed. Because love enhances flow, when we love all of our emotions come easier and we use our energy-in-motion well.

Love begins in the center of the chest—the psycho-emotional "heart"—and radiates outward, sending beams of love-energy in all directions, as from an inner star. When we love we glow with a sparkling light, sometimes visible to others, and we move and act within this halo or aura of love-energy. For this reason we can accurately speak of being *in* love. Love permeates and surrounds us like a luminous womb or cocoon, protecting and nurturing and encouraging life.

For all of its benefits to the lover, love always seeks a beloved. Love must extend outward into meaningful connection with others, must reach to bring others "in love." Love must touch, must caress, must feed and nurture, must uplift and inspire. True love flows without discrimination or conditions. Love-energy radiates through all of the self-made boundaries—the body's armor, the mind's prejudices—and causes, however temporarily, the blessed experience of true oneness. For those who sustain such love the boundaries forever dissolve, allowing the continuing experience of love to grow ever stronger, to spread to others, to become the common currency of all relationships.

Love makes things whole. Love flows as masculine energy: extending vigorously, entering into others, filling and inspiring. Love flows as feminine energy: reaching to caress, surrounding and enfolding others, protecting and nurturing. Love takes our divided and disparate selves, victims of incessant human conflict, and makes us whole people, wholly alive.

Two or more people flowing in love experience the very best aspects of being human. Connected via love-energy they may move as one, may breathe as one, may dream and create as one. When lovers touch, their hands and fingers fill with the most healing energy in the universe. Lovers' thoughts and feelings flow easily from one to the other through love-energy threads, enabling compassion, empathy, and telepathy. And when true lovers make love their union evokes the most exquisite of pleasures, effects the most profound of healings, and may even create a brand-new, love-inspired human being.

Love ever subsists as the primary matrix out of which all living relationship happens. Any relationship succeeds or fails to the degree that love flows or fails to flow. Without love-energy—extending and connecting—we live as solitary individuals, profoundly alone in the universe and essentially unrelated to all people, including family and friends.

Yet such lack of love describes the daily lives of most men and women. "Why?" we must ask. Why fail to love when its absence hurts so much? Why *not* love when loving gives so much? How do we take something so fundamental to human existence and make it so difficult, so scary, so utterly impossible? Love is the most sublime of human experiences: think of young lovers dancing on air; think of any parent gazing upon a sleeping child; think of one's feelings upon the death of an old family pet. How does something so great get twisted into the all-too-common feelings of betrayal, intolerance, avoidance, hatred, and fear?

For all its power, love cannot flow through an individual riddled with and crippled by chronic suppression. Every act of emotional suppression contracts our inflowing emotional energy and thus diminishes our experience of energy-expanding love. The more we condition our children to emotional suppression, the less love-able they become. The more we, as adults, sustain our personal patterns of suppression, the less we can feel love, the less we can teach love to our children, and the less likely they will be to teach love to their children. And so it happens that most people come to experience love as rare and difficult, rather than omnipresent and easy.

It helps to think of your emotional energy as a flowing river, circulating through all parts of your body and then gushing out beyond the body—as love—and drenching others. Your whole emotional experience arises from the one flowing river of energy. Suppress any part of the river and all of your emotions—inward flowing and outward expanding—must suffer. Suppress any feelings of sadness and your capacity for love diminishes. Suppress any feelings of anger and your capacity for love diminishes. Suppress any emotion—positive or negative, easy or difficult—and your whole emotional experience, including and especially your capacity for love, diminishes.

Yet while damming up any part of your emotional river has a suppressing effect on the whole river, freeing up any part of the river has the opposite effect. Any time you move from suppression to flow it increases the circulation of emotional energy throughout all parts of yourself. Moreover, as philosophers and poets have been telling us for ages, outward expansion of your emotional energy—as through the feelings of compassion, empathy, curiosity, and love—causes the most direct and efficacious movement to systemwide emotional flow.

Further good news: We can learn to purposefully and intentionally *practice* love. Love must become more than something that just happens to us, if we get lucky, or that we fall into and out of according to some unfathomable whimsy. We can and must learn to actively make love: to cause love-energy to stir and swell and flow out into meaningful connection with others; to gratefully open to and receive love whenever it comes our way; and to create with others a world in which such conscious loving is the sole abiding reality.

—◄o►—

Radiant Heart Breath

Now, even as you read, bring attention to the movement of your breath.

Breathe in deeply through your nose, filling your torso,

And breathe out through the mouth in a long, soft, gentle sssshhhh. . . .

Again, breathe in deeply through your nose, filling your torso,

And breathe out through the mouth in a long, soft, gentle sssshhhh. . . .

Now, continuing with this breathing, feel or sense or imagine that as you inhale

Energy flows into and fills your heart, the center of your chest,

And as you exhale the energy radiates out from the heart in all directions. . . .

Inhaling, your heart fills with energy,

Exhaling, the energy radiates out from the heart, as light from a star. . . .

Continue with several long slow gentle heart breaths,

And as you breathe think about or remember some person whom you deeply love. . . .

Let this breathing into and from the heart become a gentle movement of love-energy.

Inhaling, your heart fills with love-energy,

Exhaling, love-energy radiates out from the heart, as light from a star. . . .

Continue with several long slow gentle heart breaths,

Filling with love-energy, radiating love-energy,

Even as you read. . . .

7

Relational Inheritance

We find ways to fix [our children] so that the peculiar, generally joyless, dronelike work of Civilization will be not only bearable but actually sought after, so that they will turn even from their own bodies and beings to do this work. We find ways at the same time to dull their feelings so that they will not know what they are doing to the world outside their skins. . . . The conditions of Civilization being what they are, in fact, we might demonstrate concern for our children most convincingly by completely excising their sensitivity in this regard.

—George Leonard, *The Transformation*

Though most people never marry their mothers or murder their fathers, we all have much to learn from sad Mr. Oedipus. From the details of his tragic life we can glean two timeless truths: The relationship between our parents provides our first model for interpersonal relationship, and the relationships that we, as individuals, develop with our mothers and fathers generate the primary patterns through which all our relationships will develop.

Just as the meeting and mixing of parental genes gives every child a physical template through which the great energy-into-mass conversions of gestation, birth, and childhood development occur, so the meeting and mixing of the parental and child-parent relationships gives a child the psychoemotional templates through which the meaning and practice of "relating to others" develop. While genetic inheritance for the most part governs physical characteristics, *relational inheritance* influences emotional and mental characteristics, such as attitudes, biases, prejudices, moods, attractions, sense of humor, learning styles, and basic patterns of suppression, expression, and flow.

Relational inheritance ultimately derives from one's whole human environment, including parents and grandparents, siblings, other relatives, playmates, teachers, and any significant caregivers. Anybody who spends meaningful time with a child contributes to his or her understanding and practice of relationship. Yet the parents come first and will always register most significantly as a child develops. Even an absent parent communicates powerfully about the nature of relationship and may influence a child more than the most conscientious and loving of nonparental caregivers.

The first layer of relational inheritance comes from the relationship between the parents. From birth forward the parental relationship provides an active and ever-present model of how people relate. Like an epic drama unfolding before a small, private audience, the setting, story, dialogue, action, and meaning of the parental relationship become psychoemotional fodder for the ever-watchful and always learning child.

For the child every aspect of the parental relationship

literally matters: it *makes material*. The parents' thoughts, feelings, dreams, and behaviors, their patterns of suppression, expression, and flow, the way they feel about and act toward one another—all of it matters profoundly to the child, for all of it contributes to the child's development. The various issues that define any relationship between two adults become the core definitions of their child.

Do the parents love each other? Do they seem happy together? Does their home feel happy? Do they sing? dance? laugh? make love? How do they make decisions? *Who* makes the decisions? Who carries out which aspects of the child's care? How do the parents deal with conflict? Do they argue? Do they physically fight? Do they show each other physical affection? How do they deal with work and money? How do they move out into the world and relate to others?

However mundane daily life may seem to the parents, it all unfolds like a personal Genesis tale for their child. The parents carry on—playing, laboring, relating—in their child's Eden, the sole progenitors of this new human world. The child watches, listens, learns, and remembers. Everything the child will ever feel and think about relationship begins in and grows from the parental garden.

As the child moves through childhood and adolescence into adulthood, the parents forever exist as the model of relationship, whether the child chooses to emulate the model or to rebel against it. The child cannot escape it: the parental relationship weaves itself into his or her psyche. The child can only accept it, perhaps feel grateful for it, and ultimately learn from it and evolve.

A second deeper layer of relational inheritance comes from the child's unique relationship with each parent. Like adding color to a black-and-white sketch, the child-parent relationships take the model of the parental relationship as their point of departure but then develop beyond it. The parental relationship strongly influences the child-parent relationships, which in turn strongly influence all of the child's future relationships.

Mother and father serve the child as first woman and first man, as first playmates, companions, and friends, as first teachers, doctors, authority figures, and Supreme Beings, as first rivals, adversaries, and violators, and, especially, as first loves. Even absent parents may fill some of these roles for years. As the principal characters in the first and longest-term relationships in a child's life, the parents inculcate their child with *the* ways of relating to others during specific situations and events. Daily, continuous relationship with each parent settles into regular patterns through which the child meets, perceives, reacts to, and relates with any new person.

The child-parent relationship begins at conception. The fetus grows from the tiniest speck of matter contained within a radiant field of vital energy. Both the material speck and the radiant field derive from parental gifts at conception. Yet while the physical body of the fetus develops separately from the father and moves inexorably toward separating from the mother, the energy fields connecting the fetus and both parents remain vital and meaningful through gestation and birth and beyond.

The fetus develops as pulsing, flowing energy-in-motion nested within the pulsing, flowing energy-in-motion of its mother and outwardly connected to the pulsing, flowing energy-in-motion of its father. The parents' psychoemotional energies communicate dynamically with the psycho-emotional energies of their child. Indeed, the energetic connections between mother, father, and child have such vitality and importance that from conception through birth the child exists as almost a triune being, a mother-father-child;

whole and unavoidably honest feelings pass directly from parents to fetus, setting the tone of and laying the foundations for lifelong relationships.

Did the parents conceive the child through an act of love or through an "accident" or through an act of violence? Do both parents want the child? Do they want to become parents? Do they want a boy? A girl? Does gender matter? Can the parents afford the child or do they feel the child's coming as a financial burden? Does the family home pulse with the energy of human happiness and warm welcome, or does it reverberate with argument and tension and dread? All of these issues powerfully affect the living energies of the parents and thus the development of the fetus.

From birth forward, the child-parent relationships come into ever-sharper focus. The impact of each parent's relationship with the child only grows stronger as the child plays a more active role in the family drama. The child arrives—a brand new "center of the universe"—and its parents circle about in tight orbit, giving attention, protection, nurturance, and love. The style and quality of this parental circling impresses upon the child as the very essence of human relationship.

Did the father share in the preparation for birth, and did he attend the delivery? What decisions do the parents make regarding medical care, breast-feeding, sleeping arrangements, daily child care, and education? How do the parents respond to the child's regular crises of hunger, wet diapers, and loneliness? How do the parents touch and hold the child? How do they express affection for the child? How do they express (or deal with) anger, frustration, and disappointment with the child? And, especially, do they condition the child's emotional responses mostly toward expression, suppression, or flow?

Raising a child involves an unending series of challenges and choices and thus, for each parent, a continuous generating of energy-in-motion. The way that each parent actively and emotionally responds to the always challenging child *becomes* the always-changing world of the child. The parents' psychoemotional states, including their patterns of behavior, communication, and relationship, present an unending series of challenges to the child, who naturally answers by generating the energy-in-motion of effective response. Taken together, and repeated continuously, this interplay of the parents' energy-in-motion with the child's energy-in-motion—each forever feeding into and feeding off the other—evolves into the child's primary patterns of human relationship.

Every woman the child meets initially feels like *mother* and triggers a series of internal and external reactions that all began with the actual mother. Every man the child meets initially feels like *father* and triggers a similar, but father-defined, series of reactions. As new people take specific roles in the child's life—as teachers, caregivers, friends, and others—the child's initial reactions generally stem from previous experiences with his or her parents in such roles. While new relationships always have the potential to develop uniquely, the fact remains that both parties come parentally conditioned to specific psychoemotional patterns of interaction.

Most people never grow beyond their parent-child relationships. Rather than respond to life's challenges freely—which requires that they perceive people and events free of past conditioning—they see everything through the psychoemotional lenses of childhood. They never step free of their relational inheritance and thus can neither develop freely nor ever feel free.

To meet the world openhearted and open-minded—to live free—we must touch, move through, and finally resolve all psychoemotional patterns of the past. We must understand

and then undo the patterns of relationship we inherited from our parents. This can seem a monumental task. To go directly and literally to the heart of the matter we must first learn (again) to love freely.

Most of all, parents teach children to love. Or parents condition their children to specific patterns of feeling and not feeling love, depending on changing circumstances and the actions of other people. In fact, in one of the great conundrums of human existence parents mostly teach children *not* to love.

Babies arrive as love incarnate: loose bundles of flesh imbued with a beaming brightness that radiates freely to one and all. Babies love wholly and indiscriminately; their emotional energies expand vigorously into connection with people, animals, and plants, as well as inanimate objects. They reach with their vital energies to touch and taste and even ingest everything and everybody. More than anything, babies yearn to feel connected—to sustain psychophysical bonds with one or more caregivers—and they rage against disconnection within moments of feeling it.

True, babies live a preverbal and developmentally immature existence. They do not yet experience "I" as separate and different from "Thou," and thus their love has a quality altogether different from mature love. Yet we make a great mistake to discount, dismiss, or fail to learn from babies' love. Like little Buddhas, babies love purely, beatifically, and free of all the twists and tangles that will eventually complicate their relationships. Every baby recreates Eden—loving with perfect innocence—until seduced by parental conditioning into the world of contracted love and emotional suppression.

Most parents seem to recognize, or at least feel drawn to, their children's love. Parents and other grown-ups typically experience a melting, softening, *good* feeling in the presence of babies, leading naturally to smiles, coos, and caresses. The arrival of a new baby can bring miraculous transformations in people, especially for those who have lost or forgotten their capacity for loving.

Of the many causes of the good feelings that babies arouse—their cuteness, their helplessness, their innocence, their place on the family tree, their role in pregnancy and birth, their fulfillment of past longing, and their promise for the future—nothing affects us as deeply as the radiant fields of love-energy that envelop and extend from their bodies. Parents easily (though not always) experience love-energy bonds with their babies—bonds that have the potential to sustain the relationship over the course of a lifetime. Potentially, the child-parent relationships can bring love's continuous blessings to parents and child, while also revealing the ways to best love others. Every new baby comes into the world like a love-flame that may grow into a wondrous incandescence, spreading everywhere, if the parents will only do their part and tend the fire well.

Unfortunately, even the most loving parents have difficulty meeting the challenge. The simple act of loving their child becomes intensely problematic as multiple factors conspire against the child-parent relationship. What begins as a natural event—love-energy flowing freely between parent and child—slowly, sometimes suddenly, evolves into the complex unease and pleasure-pain entanglement that characterizes so much of family life.

From the outset, parents must contend with their own relational inheritance. Parents tend to condition their children as their own parents conditioned them. Certain patterns of relationship, including and especially the capacity for love, pass from generation to generation as surely as race or the colors of eyes and hair. Children learn to love as their parents learned and, in most families, there the story ends. Like a broken record, human history resounds with the endless repeating of sad and tragic tales of love gone wrong. Most people never recognize the causal force of relational inheritance, much less their ability (and responsibility) to pass new and liberating lessons on to the next generation.

Yet even when we work our way somewhat free of relational inheritance, staying fully *in love* with our children proves a daunting task. We find it fatiguing to remain always open and vulnerable in the way that a healthy flow of love-energy requires. We stagger through the difficult feelings that any intimate relationship must arouse; we become so consumed with anger, grief, or fear that we can hardly find our way back to love again. We place conditions on our love—I will love you if you clean your room, if you practice your lessons, if you love me back—and then we wonder why our love has failed. We try to love exclusively—loving just our children, our family, our group—then run afoul of the inevitable consequences of suppressing love around so many others.

We especially stumble over any feelings of bodily—yes, sexual—pleasure when with our children. The movement of sexual energy occurs quite naturally as we play and snuggle with these beautiful people for whom we already feel such energy-flowing love. Nursing mothers sometimes feel sexual arousal, as do many parents when bouncing children on their laps, or giving baths, or cuddling together at bedtime, or observing young bodies as they move into and through adolescence.

While we might feel grateful for such positive flows of pleasure-energy and for the relationships that inspire such feelings, for most people feeling sexual arousal in the presence of children initiates a terrible crisis. We consider the feelings wrong, if not evil, and we react as we typically react to any unwanted feelings: we unconsciously suppress the energy or, failing that, we express it. Unfortunately, both suppression and expression come with serious consequences to our children, ourselves, and all our relations.

Expressing sexual feelings with a child, from mild seductions to outright incest, always harms the child. For adults to allow their strongest and most vital energies to engulf and contaminate a child with inevitable feelings of shame, guilt, and forced submission constitutes the worst of child abuse. That adults often engage in such abuse under the guise of love further darkens the act: what a terrible message to send to a child, to equate compulsive adult weakness with love. As strong and pleasurable as the love-energy we share with our children may become, clear limits to the expression of that energy do exist. Parents must take responsibility for recognizing the limits and steadfastly honoring them.

Yet if we do not express our pleasure-feelings with our children, we hardly do better to suppress the feelings. When we suppress sexual energy in the presence of a child we stifle our inward-moving energies and, most critically, we withdraw our outward-expanding fields of love-energy. We disconnect from the child. If we have been frightened enough by the "sinful" arousal of sexual energy, we might never fully connect with the child again. We might never again risk wholebody, energy-flowing love with this child or anybody else.

The child learns that love never lasts; that, at best, he or she might hope for occasional—rare and special—moments of feeling love. The child learns that even the most intimate relationships work best if everybody keeps his or her vital energies withdrawn and safely in check. The child learns that pleasure—that wonderful sensation she or he felt just before the love went away—only brings trouble. Contrary to innate human design—to the very essence of being wholly human—the child learns to love less.

"Love!" our children sing to us. "Discover the joys of wide-open energy expansion."

"Love less," we answer back. "Tone it down, hold it in. Learn to think of love as something rare, fragile, and fleeting."

And so we condition our children away from love, away from feeling, and away from free-flowing energy-in-motion. By the time they reach puberty and the challenge of forming new and increasingly intimate relationships, most children have been conditioned (like their parents) to deeply ingrained patterns of emotional suppression and expression that will influence every moment of their unfolding lives. These patterns of relational inheritance utterly define children, so much so that they come to think of their parental conditioning as natural and innate: "It's just the way I am."

In fact, our true, unconditioned self always resides, however imprisoned, within psychoemotional patterns taken on from other people, starting with our parents. Finding our way free of all such patterns carries us back to Oedipus and the demand that we somehow marry *and* murder both mother and father. Difficult as it seems, freedom ever beckons for those who search on. Love ever lights the way for those who must live free.

◄o►

Healing Mother Breath

Now, even as you read, bring attention to the movement of your breath.

Breathe in deeply through your nose, filling your torso,

And breathe out through the mouth in a long, soft, gentle sssshhhh. . . .

Again, breathe in deeply through your nose, filling your torso,

And breathe out through the mouth in a long, soft, gentle sssshhhh. . . .

Now, continuing with this breathing, feel or sense or imagine that as you inhale

Energy flows into and fills your heart, the center of your chest,

And as you breathe out the energy radiates out from the heart in all directions. . . .

Inhaling, your heart fills with love-energy,

Exhaling, love-energy radiates out from the heart, as light from a star. . . .

Continue with several long slow gentle heart breaths. . . .

Now, as you breathe, think about or remember your mother.

Imagine that you can accept your mother into your heart

And into the gentle flowing movement of love-energy. . . .

Whatever thoughts, feelings, or memories your mother may arouse,

Continue this gentle heart-breathing, this gentle flowing love-energy,

As you simply and fully accept your mother. . . .

Gentle heart-breathing, gentle flowing love-energy,

Simply and fully accepting your mother with each breath.

Continue with several long, slow, gentle heart breaths,

Filling with love-energy, radiating love-energy, feeling acceptance,

Even as you read. . . .

8

Social Viruses

What is not used becomes obsolete—whereas what is opposed is kept before you. Therefore, the creative principle of change is the relaxed inspection and awareness of existing tendencies, and persistent, full feeling-orientation to right, new, regenerative functional patterns.

—Adi Da Samraj, *The Enlightenment of the Whole Body*

"Imagine a group of tribes living within reach of one another. If all choose the way of peace, then all may live in peace. But what if all but one choose peace?" So asks Andrew Bard Schmookler at the beginning of his study of social evolution, *The Parable of the Tribes*. As he makes clear, once one of the tribes chooses violence over peace then all of the other tribes eventually find it impossible to continue living peacefully. Once one tribe takes on social patterns of domination, aggression, and physical force, those patterns spread to all of the other tribes.

Consider the options of a tribe facing impending invasion: they can arm themselves and fight back; they can submit to and become absorbed by the invader; they can form strategic alliances with other tribes; or they can become refugees, leaving home in search of some better place. In every case, the basic nature of the tribe undergoes profound change. It can no longer stay put and act in its previously peaceful ways; rather, it finds its perceptions of the world and its reactions to events driven by the exigencies of "kill or be killed, enslave or be enslaved, dominate or be dominated." The allocation of tribal resources will shift to building defenses and stockpiling weapons. The status of warriors in the tribe will rise as tribal decision making and leadership become war driven. Over time, the mythos of the tribe will change—its stories and legends, its philosophical underpinnings, its songs, its art. All aspects of tribal identity will take on the harsher tones of domination, aggression, and warrior culture.

For individual members of the tribe, the political turns personal. Since men have greater aptitude for violence and war—being bigger, stronger, flush with testosterone, and unencumbered by pregnancy, birth, and nursing babies—the status of men as a group rises over women as a group in warrior culture. This alters the primary relationship between man and woman, between husband and wife, and thus alters the very nature of the family. The family as "peaceful partnership" gets twisted into a domination-based construct, with men on top and in charge and given to violently forcing the submission of women and children. After several generations, this pattern becomes the prime currency of all relational inheritance; people become so deeply conditioned to domination, aggression, and physical force as to think and accept, "This is human nature. This is just the way we are."

What begins as a poorly resolved conflict between social groups turns over time into a specific pattern of relationship that acts like a virulent contagion—a social virus—loose in the world and spreading everywhere. We can call this particular pattern of relationship the *dominism virus,* for it spreads the notion that all human relationship must resolve into "those who dominate" and "those who submit." Once the dominism virus enters into a relationship equation, participants find themselves compelled toward either domination or submission. Because of its long presence in human affairs and its easy movement into family dynamics, the dominism virus has insinuated its way into and debased most human relationships.

Yet however natural domination may come to feel, and however we explain, justify, and accept its large role in human affairs, we do not begin life as compulsively dominant or submissive creatures. We enter this world naturally inclined toward cooperation, partnership, and love. As we grow we take on patterns of relationship—first from parents and family, and then from key social groups—that condition, infect, and ultimately undermine our basic natures. The passing of relationship patterns from social group to individual somewhat resembles the passing of biological and computer viruses, and thus the term *social virus.*

Like biological and computer viruses, social viruses consist of quantities of information contained within unique structures that allow for reproduction and movement from one host body to another. A social virus encapsulates specific information about human relationship within a matrix of emotional energy. The energy provides the subtle yet substantial body of the virus, as well as its means of spreading.

As a social virus spreads to and infects new people, it insinuates its information into their perceptual processes and thus essentially alters the way they experience themselves and their world. Like the green glasses worn by the residents of the city of Oz—which gave the Emerald City its omnipresent green glow—social viruses color our perceptions of reality so completely that eventually we cannot differentiate human nature tainted by viral effects from human nature as it was before the virus. Indeed, after a long enough time people will vigorously defend their virus-infected lives as God-given, socially proper, or genetically determined, or some combination of the three.

Consider, for example, the social virus of racism. We see no evidence of racial prejudice in young children. The typical child, when introduced to a new playmate of some other race, will either not notice the difference in skin color or see it as a curiosity. People must encounter and succumb to a specific racial virus (they come in all colors) before they will perceive racial differences as negative. Whether an affected individual becomes prejudiced against one race in particular or against all other races depends on the relationship patterns of the social group that passes the virus. Whether an individual becomes bitterly racist or only mildly prejudiced depends on his or her preexisting patterns of relationship and subsequent life experiences. In either case the individual comes to feel his or her racial prejudices as innate, absolute, and unchanging.

Without its body of emotional energy a social virus consists of mere information. Like a monotone reading of a dry statistical analysis, information without emotion has little creative or destructive power. Even deeply pernicious information will barely register for most people—because it won't *feel* right or important—much less will it alter anyone's perceptions or behavior. To actually change people the information must become energized; it must have its own subtle yet substantial structure of emotional charge.

Think of Hitler delivering his "final solution" to the masses, or a lover proposing marriage. Or consider the loaded energy in so much of modern advertising. Information delivered with a strong emotional charge not only affects human behavior, it sinks deeply into the human psyche and alters human nature. Information without emotional charge may or may not spur one toward some new thinking that could eventually change one's experience of the world. Information infused with emotional charge has the power to immediately, deeply, and irrevocably affect one's sense of self and perceptions of reality.

Once infected with a social virus the individual may act as a carrier of the virus to others. People spread social viruses through their actions and communications; any interaction that arouses strong emotional energy—any situation that feels charged—provides a potent medium for the spread of a virus. Social viruses cross the void between two or more people on the expanding and connecting energies of such emotions as fear, anger, hate, envy, and lust, as well as the more pleasant emotions of love, compassion, and sexual desire. Like driftwood in fast-moving streams, social viruses ride the waves of vital human emotion. They will enter into and infect any exposed and vulnerable human host.

For all their creative and destructive power social viruses organize around a single compelling idea. The dominism virus holds that human conflict inevitably leads to the forceful exertion of one's will against another. Once the dominism virus spreads it becomes difficult for people to see or even imagine the peaceful resolution of challenging conflicts. Rather, they perceive that "it's a dog-eat-dog world" and that people must always aggressively compete for their basic needs; these beliefs make a certain amount of violent struggle inevitable. This simple idea—human conflict leads inevitably to violence—so colors the perceptions of people that contrary notions of cooperation, peace, and nonviolent conflict resolution seem naive, romantic, and foolish.

The racism virus convinces people that they can judge one another, mostly for the worse, by the color of their skin. Once the racism virus spreads it becomes difficult to see or even imagine people of different races living together as equals. Rather, people project specific flaws upon entire races (they're lazy, they're dishonest, they're stupid, they smell bad), and all thoughts of racial harmony turn into hopeless fantasy.

The sexism virus puts forth the idea of the natural superiority of men over women in matters of intelligence and governance. Once the sexism virus spreads it becomes difficult to see or even imagine women and men coexisting as free and equal partners. Rather, sexist families, social institutions, and systems of governance divide into fixed male and female roles that ultimately stifle and restrict both genders.

The monotheism virus maintains that one and only one God exists and He forbids the belief in any other gods. Once the monotheism virus spreads it becomes difficult for people to see or even imagine any spiritual belief, practice, or discipline other than their own as legitimate. Indeed, those infected with monotheism tend to view other beliefs as blasphemous and evil; or, at the very least, they view people who hold those beliefs as tragically misguided and in need of "saving." Throughout human history, when- and wherever monotheists have encountered "nonbelievers," great upheavals have invariably resulted as the virulent infection of "one and only one God" swept in to convert or eradicate the other-believing cultures. In some places monotheistic infection has ironically induced the very worst of human behavior.

Similarly, the scientism virus propagates the idea that the scientific process provides the only true way to perceive and comprehend reality. As scientism spreads its proponents vigorously deride and attempt to eradicate any conflicting non-scientific worldviews. The ancient and often profound wisdom of indigenous peoples, the sometimes inexplicable abilities of shamans, witch doctors, faith healers, seers, and psychics, and even long-tested systems such as yoga, ayurvedic medicine, acupuncture, and homeopathy—all such experience, as the scientism virus spreads, is labeled and dismissed as ignorance, superstition, and quackery.

The nationalism, patriotism, and unilateralism viruses all more or less hinge on the idea of my country right or wrong and *über alles*. The xenophobia virus posits that we must stand apart from and fight against all strangers and outsiders. The homophobia virus contains the same idea focused specifically on homosexuals. The competition virus infects with the idea that success in life derives only from winning over others.

While some social viruses, such as racism and xenophobia, bring nothing but suffering and limitation to the human experience, most carry a mixed bag of negative and positive effects. Dominism ultimately directs us toward violence, but along the way it can promote the engaging competitions in schoolyards and among sports teams, the hard-won achievements of businesspeople, and even the successful passing on of genes. While monotheism unleashes God's own fury against other-believers, it also has spread many of the genuine blessings of Judaism, Christianity, and Islam. Scientism has brought and continues to bring profound benefits from its incisive pursuit of knowledge; yet for every new avenue of thought that scientism opens it arrogantly dismisses and closes forever several others. The patriotic fervor and heart-thumping pride of extreme nationalism has at times been the only force that could stand in the way of such evils as Nazi Germany, itself an example of extreme nationalism gone awry.

Some social viruses never spread beyond cultural boundaries. Superstitions, for example, can take on all the fervor of religious belief and the absolute conviction of scientism within a specific culture and yet appear obviously silly to any outsiders. The germinal ideas of most superstitions—a voodoo curse can kill you; seeing a black cat causes misfortune; the number thirteen brings bad luck—carry effective meaning only within the context of specific times and places.

Similarly, many customs and mores spread only locally. Regional dialects and group jargon, for instance, will spread to and influence the communications of all new speakers in any given locale, even as they learn "proper" language in school. Various behavioral patterns—such as table manners or the interactions between those of different classes—carry all the weight and power of divine revelation, but only within a region or culture.

Other social viruses have short but terribly potent lives. Most famous, the Y2K virus of the 1990s took the idea of a worldwide computer crash predicted for New Year's Day of 2000, wrapped it in a bevy of fear-induced scenarios, and managed to infect millions of people. A few days into January 2000 Y2K disappeared from the world like a fleeting dream. The Spanish Inquisition, the Salem witch trials, and many stock market panics have followed the same pattern: one fear-wrapped idea gets loose in the mass consciousness, virulently spreads, and literally drives people crazy until finally it vanishes, leaving many shaking their heads, thinking, "What came over us?" Similarly, though of less import, most fashion crazes and fads, as well as advertising and political campaigns, can spread their singular notions throughout culture and often compel great shifts in human behavior, but only for limited time periods.

Ultimately, we can measure the success of any social virus by how long it lives and how widely it spreads. The most successful social viruses, such as dominism, sexism, monotheism, and xenophobia, all owe their capacities for living on and spreading wide to a certain quality of absoluteness. When the germinal idea of a social virus posits an arrant and unqualified belief about people and their world, then the absolute nature of that belief lends great powers of virulence. Indeed, we might think of absolutism as a key strand of DNA or vibration of energy wound into the core of some social viruses, making them near invincible in the face of competing ideas and would-be cures.

The absolute essence of dominism—in any conflict, one either dominates or submits—has throughout history rendered impotent more variable beliefs in equality, tolerance, and nonviolent negotiation. We see examples of this every day. In any of the world's war-torn regions most of the people desperately want peace. But it takes only a small group committed to violence, or even a single man with a gun, to derail the most ardently and painstakingly pursued peace processes. The absolutism of "do it my way or die" ever trumps the fractional and intricately layered work of making peace.

Likewise, the "one and only God" of monotheism for millennia has trumped the countless variants of pantheism. While monotheism demands that "Thou shalt have no others," most other-believing cultures remain open to new gods and shifting beliefs and may even welcome the evangelistic agents of monotheistic infection. The unquestioning "every woman in her place" of sexism has long made it near impossible for women (and men) to move beyond specific roles in society. The "trust absolutely no outsiders" of xenophobia generally defeats a people's best efforts at tolerance, diversity, and multiculturalism. And the "one true way to knowledge" of scientism sweeps away any more relativistic and subjectively grounded paths to the truth.

With the passing of time these social viruses have taken

on the appearance and feel of absolute truth, of innate human nature, of God's own plan. Their powers of virulence become self-fulfilling and -affirming forces; by the very fact that dominism, sexism, monotheism, and scientism exert such influence throughout so much of our world (and notice how well they go together, reinforcing one another), they obviously describe the true nature of reality and human existence. Since less absolute beliefs, behaviors, and institutions have not spread so virulently, they obviously contain false, failed, and obsolete notions.

To some extent social viruses appear indistinguishable from patterns of relational inheritance. Both subsist as specific thoughts about the human experience incorporated within charged fields of emotional energy. Both move into and condition (or infect) people on the currents of shared emotional energy that characterize daily human interactions. Both take on the sense of "real human nature" once rooted within an individual. Both most easily spread to young people, first through the family and then through society's key institutions.

Yet social viruses differ from patterns of relational inheritance in several ways. Relational inheritance moves within the milieu of the personal; social viruses traverse the political. While relational inheritance develops uniquely within each family, social viruses infect large groups of unrelated people (though family members often act as primary carriers). Relational inheritance delivers a complex tapestry of human life, including a minutia of gestures, mannerisms, and behavioral quirks, the thousand and one details of family history, and the deeply personal lifestyles of the parents; social viruses typically consist of a single simple yet especially incisive idea. Patterns of relational inheritance spread only within the family, from one generation to the next, and with inevitable alterations over time. Social viruses can exist unchanged for thousands of years, spreading everywhere and growing stronger with every new generation.

In some cases a social virus merges with relational inheritance: the political becomes the personal. The dominism virus, the oldest and most pernicious of social viruses, has infected human reality for so long that its effects run from the grand sweep of international affairs to the most intimate of individual relations. Parents pass dominist patterns of relationship on to their children (as relational inheritance), even as society (including the family) infects the children with the dominism virus. This sinks the subversive messages of dominism even deeper into the human psyche and brings human society more tightly within its thrall.

The sexism virus has likewise become intertwined with and somewhat indistinguishable from patterns of relational inheritance. The relationship between man and woman within the family recurs within almost all social institutions. Parents condition their children with sexist patterns of relationship even as society passes on sexist infection.

Ultimately, it matters little where a specific pattern of relationship comes from or how we come to contract it. Patterns of relational inheritance and social viruses have the common effects of suppressing our emotional energies, of shadowing our true nature, of coloring our perceptions of the world, and of somewhat controlling our responses to people and events. So very much of "who we are" emanates from these unwittingly contracted contagions. Like rare gems wrapped within multiple layers of tissue and packaging, our true selves have long been enveloped by a gross film of parental and social conditioning. We cannot even think unencumbered thoughts, much less live authentic lives, unless we learn to recognize and then move beyond all such viral influences.

‐◄○►‐

Healing Father Breath

Now, even as you read, bring attention to the movement of your breath.

Breathe in deeply through your nose, filling your torso,

And breathe out through the mouth in a long, soft, gentle sssshhhh. . . .

Again, breathe in deeply through your nose, filling your torso,

And breathe out through the mouth in a long, soft, gentle sssshhhh. . . .

Now, continuing with this breathing, feel or sense or imagine that as you inhale

Energy flows into and fills your heart, the center of your chest,

And as you breathe out the energy radiates out from the heart in all directions. . . .

Inhaling, your heart fills with love-energy,

Exhaling, love-energy radiates out from the heart, as light from a star. . . .

Continue with several long slow gentle heart breaths. . . .

Now, as you breathe, think about or remember your father.

Imagine that you can accept your father into your heart

And into the gentle movement of love-energy. . . .

Whatever thoughts, feelings, or memories your father may arouse,

Continue this gentle heart-breathing, this gentle flowing love-energy,

As you simply and fully accept your father. . . .

Gentle heart-breathing, gentle flowing love-energy,

Simply and fully accepting your father with each breath.

Continue with several long, slow, gentle heart breaths,

Filling with love-energy, radiating love-energy, feeling acceptance,

Even as you read. . . .

9

Healing Relationship

*Sometimes people ask in puzzlement how or why en-
lightened masters "renounce" sex. They don't. It isn't
a matter of giving it up; sex loses its relevance. The
charge between you and everything-that-is is so much
greater than it can be between you and another little
bit of what is that sex is a damp squib in comparison.*

—JULIE HENDERSON, *THE LOVER WITHIN*

Six people have gathered around a conference table for a business meeting. Without any warning, a huge growling tiger
comes through the door. Immediately every person in the
room experiences strong surges of emotional energy—feelings of fear boiling into terror—and their bodies undergo a
rush of rapid changes. Their hearts beat faster, their mouths
open to inhale deeply, their pupils dilate and all of their senses
sharpen, their adrenal glands pump adrenaline throughout
their bodies, and their muscles contract in preparation for
action. All of this happens without a moment's thought as,
for the first few seconds, all people in the room follow their

innate design: they perceive the tiger as a threat and then generate the moving energy of empowered response.

Within seconds, however, each person behaves differently. John blurts out a terse profanity then darts for the only window in the room. Jane remains seated, frozen, unbreathing, and unable to manage even a scream. Robert does scream, loudly, and then starts throwing chairs at the tiger. Mary slips under the table and weeps quietly, pleading, "Nice tiger, pretty tiger" over and over. Harry wields his chair defensively, like a lion tamer, and corrals the tiger toward the door. Debbie settles into a calm, beaming stillness moments after the tiger has entered the room.

What accounts for the different reactions? While each person began life with the same essential design, his or her perceptions of and spontaneous reactions to the tiger derived from a lifetime of layered-in influences. Starting with the determinants of genetic constitution, then adding layers of relational inheritance, then more layers from various social viruses, and yet more layers from their personal histories of emotional expression, suppression, and flow, each person met the tiger uniquely conditioned toward a specific response.

John was born to a slight and frail body; was bullied mercilessly, first by his father and later by classmates; rarely received help, not even from his mother, with any of his problems; and became seriously infected with the "every man for himself" virus of dominism. Jane took on her mother's fear and distrust of most of the natural world, beginning with her own body; was especially affected by an unforgettable spider incident that drove her mother to hysterical screaming; developed asthma by the age of seven; and started having sporadic panic attacks as a teenager. When Robert started kindergarten, the prolonged periods of sitting still and trying in vain to process verbal information drove him into the fidgety restlessness of hyperactivity; to his parents' dismay, over the course of the next few years their sweet son transformed into a difficult, learning-disabled problem student, given to fits of rebellion and aggression; he was taught to control his "hyper energy" with Ritalin and other drugs. Mary suffered sexual and emotional abuse from both parents throughout her childhood; came to expect that the more she cried the worse she would be treated and that, after all, she deserved it; and experienced enough good times with her parents to leave her forever confused over feelings of love, hate, pleasure, pain, safety, and danger. Harry learned as a child to believe in his basic instincts and abilities; always admired his father as a take-charge man of action; and through a love of such activities as downhill skiing, rock climbing, and skydiving, came to actually crave the adrenaline rush of dangerous situations. Debbie meditated and practiced Buddhism for many years; cultivated a feeling of nonattachment to the things of this world; and worked in a hospice with dying people, which brought her to deal with and come to accept her own death.

Each person felt a similar rush of fear-energy when the tiger entered the room but then perceived the situation and used the energy—poorly or well—according to his or her own history of emotional conditioning. Those who used the fear-energy poorly acted out of unresolved emotional and behavioral patterns from childhood; indeed, they reacted *as* children. Ironically, their reactions—fleeing, freezing, raging, crying—did offer their best chances of surviving when, as children, they faced serious challenges. Children simply do not have the range of options or abilities that adults have when threatened or violated or when suffering loss. Children often must rely on less-than-ideal psychoemotional strategies—including hysteria, hallucination, desensitization, and disassociation—as their only options to effectively deal with difficult situations and people.

Unfortunately, because such strategies work—the child gets through the immediate difficulty—the child reaches for them again when he or she faces similar difficulties in the future. With time the child unconsciously adopts a whole pattern of perception and response that automatically governs behavior when certain emotions come up. If left in place these childhood patterns effectively control that person's perceptions and responses throughout life; the child becomes parent to an emotionally impaired adult.

People who tend to use their emotional energies well have received good emotional training as children or have undergone some degree of self-examination and emotional retraining as adults, or both. In the next chapter we will explore the basics of raising emotionally healthy children. Yet even the best-raised children will invariably take on some unhealthy patterns of perception and response and will need, as adults, to bring awareness to all such patterns and learn to effectively deal with emotional energies.

As we undergo such self-examination and emotional retraining, we eventually discover that all of our childhood patterns develop from our relationships with other people. Beginning with parents, siblings, teachers, and caregivers, and continuing with the viral inputs of society, the emotional patterns that so define each of us all form in relation to specific individuals or groups of people. Even seemingly impersonal events, like natural disasters, will uniquely condition a child based on how other people function during the event. (The child whose parents were at work when the earthquake struck comes away with deep feelings of abandonment; the child who was home with a family that responded courageously learns of overcoming adversity.)

Human suffering originates as damaged relationship. We become more or less estranged from other people as children and then spend our days afflicted with damaged relationship—an affliction that vitiates all aspects of our lives. Yet the source of our suffering also provides the key to our healing. Our current relationships, problematic as they have become, offer a clear and incisive opportunity to resolve the past and live freely and effectively in the present.

Emotional energy flows throughout the body in regular, life-sustaining currents and extends beyond the body in radiant, life-connecting fields. Our experience of relationship—from moment to moment and person to person—derives from the expansive vitality of our life-connecting fields of emotional energy. We feel related to others, more or less, depending on whether and how we energetically connect. When our fields of energy become suppressed, contracted, and shrunken inward, we experience disconnection from others and our relationships suffer. When our fields of energy radiate freely we move toward vital connection with others and experience enhanced relationship.

Energy serves as both the medium and the message of relationship. The omnipresent energy that fills our world provides the medium through which the energetics of relationship can occur. Just as whale songs travel great distances through ocean water, we communicate (we spread ourselves to others) through the energy matrix that encompasses all life on earth. At the same time, much of what we communicate to others consists of the patterns of energy that have come to define us. Like a radio station sending out its specific content, each of us continuously broadcasts our "message" to current and potential others. This message comes out of our interior world and may include a full panorama of thoughts, feelings, dreams, and memories. We especially communicate any fixed or contracted patterns of emotional energy, including those of relational inheritance, social viruses, and the unresolved energies of emotional suppression.

When two or more people have a relationship, they energetically "tune in" to one another's messages. For short and passing relationships—as with a checker at the grocery or a stranger on the street—this tuning in amounts to no more than the channel surfing of a bored television viewer. One picks up but a brief and vague hint of another and then moves on, with little effect. In more intimate relationships people essentially stay tuned to one another—as senders and receivers—for longer periods of time and experience. Ideally, this means that they willingly engage in a full and mutual sharing of their innermost selves, even if they do not comprehend the energy dimensions of that sharing; that they commit themselves to honest communications (truth in sending practices); and that they actively listen for the whole message of the other, from its more overt expressions to its most subtle vibrations.

This brings us to one of the great mysteries of human relationship: why do we feel attracted to certain people? While some of the explanation certainly has to do with such externals as physical appearance, social class, education, vocation, and avocations, the full story lies in the sending and receiving of subtle patterns of energy. Each of us continuously communicates specific relationship patterns formed through our unique experiences. We tend to attract those who in some way resonate with our patterns, even as we feel attracted to those whose patterns touch or trigger something within us.

As an example, a man who experienced unremitting criticism from his mother throughout childhood will embody a whole tapestry of specific memories, perceptual tendencies, personal laws, and suppressed emotional energies—a pattern of relationship—related to her stance toward him. Though he may give no thought to his mother or his childhood, the "I can never do it right" pattern of relationship will nonetheless have a strong voice in his energy message to others. He will tend to attract someone who in some way connects to that message: perhaps another harping critic (just like Mom), or another longtime recipient of harsh criticism (who can relate), or perhaps someone who always experienced loving parental acceptance (who can thus point to another way of being).

The specifics of one's personal story do not matter so much as the general meanings and emotional tones. The woman who has a problem with her father may end up working for a female boss "just like her father" or a male boss who matches the role she played in the father-child relationship. One's overprotective mother may show up in a beloved pet that inspires similar feelings of overprotectiveness or in a teacher who challenges and pushes beyond feelings of safety. The boy who grew up competing for a parent's love may turn life into a competitive struggle against everyone he meets.

We draw people to us, even as we feel drawn toward others, in part because we somehow fit together. Our stories sound some common chord. The patterns of relationship that I transmit touch the patterns that you transmit and they resonate, they resound, they cause reverberations within each of us, subtle vibrations that get our attention, that make us notice each other, that start us relating.

We especially feel attracted to those who, because of their unresolved patterns of damaged relationship, can help us to feel and ultimately heal our own unresolved patterns of damaged relationship. The people whom we feel most attracted to have a way of reaching inside and touching our suppressed emotional energies and unresolved relationship issues (which explains why "you always hurt the one you love"). This accounts for both the magical wonder and the hellish struggle of human relationship. We feel drawn together so that we can bring awareness to the patterns of contracted energy that hurt and bind (the hellish struggle) and then let go of them (the magical wonder).

The health and status of a relationship largely reflects the degree to which each person participates (or not) in this invisible play of sending and receiving emotional energies. Thus we commonly speak of people who "keep everything inside" or who "won't let others in." They seem shut down, closed, distant, withdrawn, uptight, turned off, frigid, and unfeeling. Their opposites "fill the room" with their personalities and live their lives "like open books." They have personal magnetism. They seem open, outgoing, accessible, engaging, warm, attractive, sensitive, and feeling.

When any participant in a relationship fails to send or receive, the relationship suffers. If such suffering goes on for too long, the relationship contracts into dysfunction. Conversely, when all participants at the very least make concerted efforts to stay tuned in to one another, then the relationship grows, develops, and moves toward fulfillment.

Immediately after the tiger incident, Harry and Debbie fell in love. Though they had been coworkers for several months it now seemed as if they could see each other for the first time, and they liked what they saw. Indeed, each felt a sudden strong attraction for the other that pulled them together and propelled them through the opening stages of a love affair. They became inseparable, spending all their time together, sharing life stories, likes and dislikes, long-held dreams, and even some secrets. They discovered the joys of sex, Harry moved in, and they began talking about marriage and babies.

A year or so into their relationship, however, things started to unravel. Harry liked to drink, Debbie thought, a bit too much like her alcoholic father. When she first tried to talk to Harry about his drinking he became moody and withdrawn. Later conversations triggered extreme and dangerous rages. Harry considered the "drinking thing" much ado about nothing. He found himself steadily annoyed by Debbie's constant carping on that and a slew of other issues. After a while it seemed they did nothing but argue, with intermitting bouts of vigorous sex. The time came when they both had to admit that their love had died. Harry moved out, and their relationship came to an end.

What happened? When they first fell in love Harry and Debbie experienced, as all new lovers do, an exhilarating two-way rush of emotional energies. Harry expanded outward to embrace Debbie with his energy-self, even as she energy-embraced him. Debbie opened herself to all of Harry's offerings, even as he opened to hers. They each basked in the other's light and danced to the other's song. They lived, breathed, and moved *in* the other's love-energy, as if it formed a subtle chrysalis that gave them safety, nurturance, and the promise of ecstatic transformation.

For as long as they stayed *in love*, they received a host of secondary blessings that come with love. Their bodies worked better, they felt mentally and spiritually inspired, they became healthier on all levels. Their communication skills improved immensely as they finished each other's sentences, sensed each other's aspirations, and welcomed each other's pains. The passion that they felt for each other flowed outward, touching those around them with positive energy, spreading a "love virus" throughout their world.

Yet eventually one of the blessings of living *in love* that doesn't always feel so wonderful occurred: they began to touch and arouse each other's patterns of damaged relationship. Like unwitting psychic doctors, each reached into the other, feeling for and palpating suppressed emotional energies. Their beautiful affair turned problematic and at times felt awful. Unaware of the opportunity for deep healing that had opened before them, each began to contract inward. Harry withdrew from Debbie as she withdrew from him. Debbie made herself less vulnerable to Harry as he likewise closed her out. Essentially, they energy-disconnected, their love withered, and their relationship died.

All relationships pass through periods like this, when the healing that must happen makes it nearly impossible to stay in love. Some couples manage to remain together, but only by sustaining their emotional suppression and disconnection. They devolve into dysfunctional relationships, sharing little of their true selves and not risking love, passion, or real emotional healing. Other couples call it quits. The lovers move on to find new partners who, alas, eventually trigger the same old feelings and suppressed emotional energies. The same old patterns of damaged relationship repeat with every new partner until the lovers accept the healing that must happen or give up on love altogether.

True lovers find the courage and the will to stay emotionally flowing and connected through the hard times. They keep communicating. They stay energy-alive and open to each other's message even when it hurts—*especially* when it hurts. They honor their commitments. They see love as a forever journey rather than some fairy tale destination, and they accept all the twists and turns of that journey, the sudden changes, the unexpected transformations, and the inevitable healings.

The difference between settling for a stuck and unhealthy relationship and calling it quits or creating a healthy flowing relationship comes down to each individual's emotional responses when things get difficult. Those who respond with various combinations of unaccepting attitude, chronic bodily tension, and stifled breathing inflict damage upon themselves and their relationships. Those who respond with a mix of active acceptance, dynamic relaxation, and connected breathing create for themselves and others all the positive benefits of emotional flow.

As an example, Harry and Debbie, while still deeply in love, had naturally started to trigger suppressed patterns of emotional energy in each other. For several days Debbie had been thinking about her father, remembering the bad times and seeing her father in Harry during some of his behaviors. She tried to suppress these unwanted thoughts and feelings, but the harder she tried the worse she felt and the more annoyed with Harry she became. Finally, while on their way to an important dinner party, the building tension overwhelmed her and she blurted out, "Harry, do you think you could keep your drinking under control tonight?"

Of all the ways that Debbie could have raised her concerns and of all the things she could have said, she chose (albeit unconsciously) an approach that had no chance of doing anything other than making matters worse. *Because* she had felt unable to accept her father's or Harry's behavior, *because* her body had developed some acute tensions, and *because* she had been stifling her breath for days, she had gradually become emotionally suppressed and energy-withdrawn from Harry. When she finally spoke, she did so as an unhealthy, uninspired, and unintelligent individual who had disconnected from her partner.

Unfortunately, Harry responded in like manner, saying, "Oh, great, just what every party needs, a self-righteous nag." Feeling attacked by Debbie's words, Harry defensively shrank inward and pulled his energy-self away from Debbie, as he tried to suppress all the upset thoughts and feelings that roiled within. When he reacted, he did so as an unhealthy, uninspired, unintelligent, and disconnected individual.

Harry's reaction, of course, only caused further contraction in Debbie, and more stupid words, which caused more contraction in Harry, and more stupid words, and so it went. Debbie and Harry had reached a critical crossroads in their relationship. They would either take the path of open and honest communication or stumble down the road of chronic suppression. They would either stay energy-connected and vitally related or they would pull back, close off, and settle for a halfhearted, futile attempt at relating across a widening abyss.

To create a healthy flowing relationship *somebody* has to respond with emotional flow when things get difficult. When Debbie first started to get in touch with her father feelings triggered by Harry, she could have finally accepted her father in his entirety or simply accepted that, at that point in time, Harry drank a lot. Such acceptance would not mean that she liked Harry's drinking; she could certainly hope for and even work for change in that area. Acceptance in the here and now only meant that she would stay emotionally open and energy-connected with Harry, even when he drank too much. She would respond by expanding with acceptance rather than contracting with denial.

Or, when Debbie first blurted out her criticism, Harry could have actively accepted her words and all the feeling they conveyed. This would not mean that he liked what she said, that he agreed with her opinion, or that he would change his behavior to suit her. Active acceptance would simply demand that as he heard her words he would intentionally open and energy-expand, rather than defensively shrink away. He would energy-embrace Debbie's whole message, even though (especially because) it hurt.

At the same time, Debbie and Harry both had the option of practicing dynamic relaxation. When Debbie first began to feel upset she could have taken a meditation break, gotten a massage, or engaged in some form of healing exercises, like hatha yoga or tai chi. She could have tracked and released the tensions in her body as they formed and before they drove her toward suppression and disconnection. Likewise, even while driving the car, when Harry first felt attacked by Debbie he could have listened internally to his body's reactions and consciously let go of any arising tensions. With practice they could have developed their ability to stay physically loose and to keep their internal energies flowing strong and expanding outward.

Moreover, when the difficult feelings first emerged they could have tuned in to their breathing, noticed if it felt contracted, stifled, and shrinking, and begun a gentle movement of conscious connected breathing. They could have inhaled slowly and deeply, from the lower belly all the way up to the chest and shoulders, and then, without stopping, let the breath flow out in a long slow emptying exhale, until, without stopping, the breath moved in again. By simply breathing in this way for a few minutes they would have encouraged a full and healthy emotional flow, within and without. They would have moved toward relaxation and release on all levels. And they would have directly embodied an attitude of active acceptance—I breathe it in, I breathe it out, I breathe it in again.

As with dynamic relaxation and active acceptance, conscious connected breathing works best when practiced on a regular basis. We can develop the ability to feel it *immediately* when difficult people or circumstances stifle our breathing. Rather than allow such situations to build into crises, we can immediately move away from stifling with gentle flowing breath. Truly, no person or set of circumstances has the power to stop our breathing, to cause unhealthy contraction within us, or to make us disconnect from vital relationship. We give up our power by unconsciously giving up our breath, by allowing stresses to get out of control, and by habitually saying no to people and circumstances. We can always regain our power simply by remembering to breathe fully and freely, by letting go of tensions in our bodies, and by opening to and accepting all that life offers.

Before beginning the Acceptance Breath practice, identify a current problem or difficulty in your life that you want to work with. Choose something that is causing some degree of emotional distress, from a minor annoyance to a raging upset. State the problem in a few concise words, such as, "I'm feeling stuck," "I've been gaining weight," "John won't speak to me," "I just got fired," or "My cancer is malignant." Use this to create an "acceptance statement" in the following form: "Even though [the problem], I totally accept myself."

◄○►

Acceptance Breath

Now, even as you read, bring attention to the movement of your breath.

Breathe in deeply through your nose, filling your torso,

And breathe out through the mouth in a long, soft, gentle sssshhhh. . . .

Now, continuing with this breathing, feel or sense or imagine that as you inhale

Energy flows into and fills your heart, the center of your chest,

And as you breathe out the energy radiates out from the heart

In all directions, sssshhhh. . . .

Inhaling, your heart fills with love-energy,

Exhaling, love-energy radiates out from the heart, as light from a star, sssshhhh. . . .

Continue with several long, slow, gentle heart breaths. . . .

Now, as you inhale, filling your heart, think, "Even though I . . . ," and then

As you exhale, radiating from your heart, think or say aloud, "I totally accept myself."

Every inhale, filling your heart and feeling your problem, pain, or difficulty.

Every exhale, radiating from your heart, and feeling and affirming total self-acceptance.

Every inhale, filling your heart and feeling the challenges, losses, and violations of life.

Every exhale, feeling and affirming total self-acceptance.

Every inhale, filling your heart and feeling life.

Every exhale, feeling and affirming acceptance of all of your life,

Even as you read. . . .

10

A Happy Childhood

An irony of history is that a child conceived, birthed, and brought up without restraint of any conceivable kind would never need restraining, not as a child, adolescent, or adult . . . [O]ur natural state is one of unbroken relationship with our creator, in which everything works together for good as proposed, and the natural instinct of the child is to maintain that state of relationship at all costs.

—JOSEPH CHILTON PEARCE, THE BIOLOGY OF TRANSCENDENCE

The story goes that in a long-ago kingdom there ruled an emperor who became so obsessed with appearances that he always had to wear the latest fashions. A clever thief came to the palace one day and persuaded the emperor that he could weave a new cloth so fine and exquisite that to those of unsophisticated sensibilities it would appear invisible. "Only a refined eye such as yours," the thief said to the emperor, "will be able to see the garments made from this cloth." So with much anticipation the emperor commissioned his new wardrobe.

Several days later the thief announced he had finished, and the emperor eagerly tried on his new clothes. Though the supposedly enrobed emperor stood stark naked before a mirror, he could not think of himself as too uncouth to see the cloth. Instead he perceived as he had been conditioned to perceive; he saw the finest clothing in all the land. The emperor complimented the thief on his extraordinary work and proudly showed off his new clothing to the royal family and retainers. They in turn convinced themselves of the wonder of the emperor's new clothes rather than admit that they lacked sophistication. Several members of the court even ordered new wardrobes for themselves made with the thief's fine and exquisite cloth.

They held a grand parade to celebrate and display the emperor's new clothes. As he marched naked before all his people, they too could not allow themselves to see the obvious. A swell of excited voices swept through the crowd as everyone proclaimed the majesty of the emperor's new clothes. But then, piercing through the rising din, a child's voice squealed, "The emperor's naked!" In a moment the illusion of the emperor's new clothes dissolved, and all could see the simple truth.

Like the sadly deluded emperor, each of us moves through the world cloaked in a grand illusion. We see and believe as we have been conditioned to see and believe. We perceive reality through a colored glass of parental and social conditioning; our perceptions then predispose us to responses that tend to reinforce our conditioning. This repeating loop of conditioning, perception, response, and experience defines and determines our interior and exterior realities and poorly affects all of our relationships and creative efforts. We wear these false realities throughout our lives with only fleeting, anxious glimpses of our true selves.

Just as it took a child to shatter the illusion of the emperor's new clothes, the surest path out of our shared illusion lies in the unconditioned perceptions and infinite energies of childhood. Though the pressures of emotional suppression weigh intensely on every child, it takes years to fully rein in a child's spirit. Even as the forces of relational inheritance and social conditioning gradually corrupt a child's perceptions and experiences, his or her true nature shines on with willful resolve. If we but watch our children and listen well—if we make a determined effort to comprehend the enchanted landscape of childhood—then children *will* confront us with unadorned truth.

For adults the whole notion of free-flowing emotions and expanding-connecting fields of energy can seem like a fairytale belief in magical powers. We dismiss children's reality as a never-never land. We condescend to their uninformed and immature natures. We expect them to grow up and leave their childish ways behind. We demand that sooner rather than later they conform to their conditioning and perceive, respond to, and experience the world as we do.

Yet for children energy-in-motion abides as an omnipresent force that propels their busy, nonstop bodies; that animates their toys, stuffed animals, and other objects; that inspires their epic imaginations; and that tightly bonds them to their families and friends. We can only guess what might happen if adults learned to nurture and encourage the energy-rich experiences of children. Though we fear that they would never grow up, they might instead grow into a whole new race.

The younger the child, the more vigorous the flow of emotions and the more expansive the connecting fields of energy. We might expect the opposite—that as our bodies and intellects grew, so would our energy-selves. But the journey from birth to adolescence to adulthood to death entails a gradual dampening of a child's once-infinite light, as layer upon layer of relational inheritance, emotional suppression, and social viruses takes its toll.

So people shrink with age. They contract inward, becoming tighter, compacted, brittle, and wrinkled; their emotions deaden, their sexual juices wither, and their philosophies turn rigid. All of this obvious shrinking that we take for granted as the natural and inevitable course of life begins in childhood with the unnatural and unnecessary beating down and reining in of the child's spirit.

We should expand with age. We should become lighter, more open and flexible, our emotions free-flowing, our sexual energies ever vital, and our minds bright and learning all the time. But suppressed emotional energies, patterns of relational inheritance, social viruses, and the supposed inevitabilities of growing older all hang over us, like the fabricated nonsense of a clever thief, to hide our true natures and prevent us from clearly perceiving and experiencing reality . . . until a child reveals the truth.

The framers of the American Constitution invoked a world in which all people had certain unalienable rights, including the right to "the pursuit of happiness." Unfortunately, the notion of *pursuit* implies a continuing quest with no guarantee of actual attainment. A nation pledged to the pursuit of happiness might come to think of its people primarily as consumers whose sole purpose resides in the unceasing amassing of stuff in a vain and forever frustrated chasing after happiness.

How much better if the framers had enshrined the more achievable right to a happy childhood. Imagine a world where the will of the people and the full force and treasury of the state conspire to provide every newborn baby with the essentials of a full and healthy childhood; where every child has equal and undeniable access to first-class food, shelter, health care, and education; and where We the People make it our most solemn duty to assure that all children grow up in happy, loving families.

Of course, even if the state commits (as some nations do) to providing the requisites of a full and healthy childhood, the task of providing loving families will always belong to parents (or primary caregivers). Children need parents who themselves have discovered the ways of emotional flow, expanding love, and common happiness. They need parents who understand—who celebrate, who cherish—the always moving, rushing, soaring energies of childhood. Most important, children need parents who can comprehend and then dissolve the unhealthy patterns of childhood conditioning that bedevil any family.

All parents face the challenge of resolving, for themselves and their children, a basic conundrum of human development. The repeating loop of conditioning-perception-response-experience derives from the greater repeating loop of parents passing on patterns of relationship learned as children from parents who passed on virtually identical patterns they learned as children. Each generation conditions the next, which similarly conditions the next, which similarly conditions the next. So how do we pass on to our children anything other than what our parents passed on to us? How do we *not* become our mothers and fathers? How do we nurture in our children their full and unconditioned potential?

Before we can hope to raise emotionally free and happy children we must achieve some degree of emotional freedom and happiness for ourselves. This means that parents (and other caregivers) *must* undergo their own emotional healing and retraining. Unhappy parents teach unhappiness to their children. Abusive parents teach abuse. Addicted parents teach addiction. Parents who fear intimacy teach fear of intimacy, parents who have difficulty communicating impart poor communication skills, and parents who relate badly to others spread bad relationship.

Parents cannot, nor should they want to, escape providing models for their children. Parents cannot avoid passing on patterns of relationship. Parents can and must teach and nurture themselves, grow themselves, so that, at the very least, they model an unswerving commitment to *becoming* open, honest, and loving individuals.

In the best of all possible worlds parents would do all of their self-work before they ever had children. Children and adolescents would learn the basics of living happily and relating lovingly as an essential piece of their primary education. Such boys and girls would grow into emotionally balanced men and women who would naturally pass on happiness to their own children, who would likely take the possibilities of happy loving lives to grand new levels.

For now, as we move toward such a world, we do the best we can. We practice the simple tools for encouraging emotional flow offered in this book or we find and practice similar tools. We become more accepting of others and ourselves. We learn to relax. We experience the power of free-flowing breath. We do our self-work secure in the knowledge that, to whatever degree we can find emotional health and genuine happiness for ourselves, we have created a world that much better for our children.

Until we reach that best of all possible worlds, where adults have become models of emotional flow and social conditioning has become a liberating force in human development, then we must find ways to relate to children that do as little negative conditioning as possible and that move our children and us along the path of healing. This proves to be a formidable task for most adults. Children can seem like creatures from another planet with their undeveloped speech, their perplexing questions, their unfathomable inner states, and their hyperactive (to us) emotions.

We find it easier to relate to children when we remember one thing: children still experience the world through strong, effective, and creative fields of radiant energy. They still live in emotional Eden. Though we see children as small and undeveloped, we would do better to pay attention to their large and as yet unsuppressed energy-selves.

Children essentially relate to the world via inward-moving and outward-expanding emotional energies. Thus the way that our emotional energies connect with (or fail to connect with) a child's emotional energies has far more impact upon the child than anything we say or do. Our words can sound like so much gobbledygook to a child and, no matter how hard we try to explain, our actions often baffle. But our emotional energies penetrate and impress the child in a language all children understand.

It helps to think of children as "emotion detectors." Always assume that children, even newborn babies, can and will feel the emotional transmissions of everyone in their immediate environment (and especially their parents). They do this as surely as they breathe in the surrounding air. Even when we manage to keep our true feelings from ourselves, children can accurately sense our emotional flux. Our children know, simply and directly, when we feel good and when we hurt. They know it because they *feel* it. And our children respond, naturally and inevitably, from and with their parentally affected feelings.

We feel, they resonate with what and how we feel, and

they thereby inherit from us specific patterns of emotional expression, suppression, and flow.

If after an especially bad day you walk into your house with feelings of hurt and anger roiling within, you unavoidably communicate those feelings to your children. You cannot escape this. Even if you put on your best happy face, your children will sense your true unhappiness. They will at the very least feel confused by your incongruence. Moreover, if your unhappy feelings persist your children will in some way take those feelings on for themselves—they will inherit some aspect of your unhappiness.

Yet what choices does a parent have at such times? If, on the one hand, you visibly and vocally express your unhappy feelings, then your children will naturally feel your sadness, anger, or fear coming at them as if directed toward them. Despite your best explanations—Daddy just had a bad day at work, it has nothing to do with you, I love you—your children will blame themselves for your bad feelings (just as children tend to blame themselves for their parents' divorcing, their failures at work, and their physical illnesses). If, on the other hand, you contract inward and tightly suppress your unhappy feelings, your children will experience that as a profound disconnection from a most vital other. They will feel that you have withdrawn and pulled away from them. And, again, they will blame themselves for your withdrawal.

Parents face a hard but potentially liberating truth: Your children will always take personally any negative movement of your emotional energies. Moreover, they will experience such negativity either as expressed abuse or suppressed disconnection. In either case, *they will feel unloved*. Anytime you feel sad, angry, or fearful in the presence of your children—whether you express the feelings or suppress them—your children will sense an unpleasant disturbance in your emotional energies and will begin to doubt your love. *You cannot escape this.* Your children will not perceive the circumstances contributing to your unhappiness, nor will they believe your most sincere assurances of your continuing love for them. They will experience the full emotional energetics of each moment, and they will interpret anything less than free-flowing and unconditionally loving energies from you as a lack or withdrawal of love.

This leaves parents with a simple though not always easy recipe for providing happy childhoods: *feel happy*. If we want our children to feel loved then we must experience love-energy as a vital expanding force, especially when in the presence of our children. And why stop there? This does not mean that we will not still feel and have to deal with the difficult emotions aroused by unpleasant circumstances, but that we make a firm commitment to moving as expeditiously as possible from unhealthy patterns of emotional suppression and expression to the all-accepting and loving energies of emotional flow.

Once we accept this essential formula our children become our own expert emotional trainers, our private gurus, revealing the way to emotional flow and pointing out each time we slip off the path. "The emperor has no clothes!" they shout anytime we cover our happy selves with painful patterns of the past and binding social conditioning. We have but to listen, to find the courage to change, and to practice the basic tools of emotional healing. Moreover, even as we do our self-work, we must extend our best efforts to include our children.

This means that in relation to our children, and especially when in their presence, we work toward an enduring attitude of active acceptance that covers all of our thoughts, feelings, and actions as well as all that our children say and do. We accept it all. Not that we and our children will not make mistakes, nor that everybody will not always have room for improvement, but that in the here and now we intentionally open to and accept whatever happens, just the way it happens. We accept our children and ourselves as they and we happen.

We must strive to make this all-encompassing acceptance our immediate response to whatever our children say and do. We can always offer reasoned criticisms later, after our emotions have had time to flow into balance. Any critical judgments, hard lectures, or even punishments of a child that we deem necessary will prove far more effective when delivered from a place of flowing acceptance. Mary Poppins got it right: A spoonful of sugar does make the medicine go down, just as the feeling of unconditional love—especially when your child has erred—provides the perfect environment for childhood learning and development.

We have to beware of and ultimately reject the notion that we can change our children (or anyone else) for the better by showing them how bad they have made us feel. This may rate as the all-time least successful parenting strategy. Nobody learns anything useful while feeling assaulted by another's unhappiness. While we may in effect bully our children into altering their behavior with our dangerous rants and our dark and smoldering moods, while we may even think that we can pick up the rod and beat some sense into them, in fact, such tactics only teach disconnection and abuse as primary patterns of relationship.

Children learn love when they experience our unconditional love. They learn happiness when we feel happy. They learn open, honest, and accepting relationship when we relate to them with openness, honesty, and acceptance.

Anytime your child upsets or worries you, first take a deep breath. Then as you continue with a gentle, flowing breath, center yourself in the heart, turn on the feeling of love, and extend your energies to touch and embrace your child. Feel, sense, or imagine yourself as radiant flowing energy that surrounds your child with protection, encouragement, and healing. Sustain this breathing, loving, energy-in-motion connection with your child for as long as either of you feels disturbed.

With time and practice, this breathing-love pattern of relationship takes the place of less beneficial patterns. It becomes our first response to most of life's changes, as natural as breath, as easy as first love, and as creative as infinite energy in eternal motion. Practice, practice, practice. We have nothing to lose but our unhappiness. We have everything to gain.

Before beginning the Wisdom Breath practice, identify a personal or relationship question that you would like help with, such as "What is the source of my current anger?" "Can I really trust Bob?" "How do I deal with my child's willfulness?" "How can Mary and I improve our sex life?" "What is my purpose in life?"

◄o►

Wisdom Breath

Now, even as you read, bring attention to the movement of your breath.

Breathe in deeply through your nose, filling your torso,

And breathe out through the mouth in a long, soft, gentle sssshhhh. . . .

Now, continuing with this breathing, feel or sense or imagine that as you inhale

Energy flows into and fills your heart, the center of your chest,

And as you breathe out the energy radiates out from the heart

In all directions, sssshhhh. . . .

Inhaling, your heart fills with love-energy,

Exhaling, love-energy radiates out from the heart, as light from a star, sssshhhh. . . .

Continue with several long slow gentle heart breaths. . . .

Now, as you inhale, filling your heart, ask your question, and then as you exhale,

Radiating from your heart, feel total self-acceptance while opening to an answer. . . .

Every inhale, filling your heart and feeling your question,

Every exhale, radiating from your heart,

Feeling self-acceptance, and listening for answers. . . .

Every inhale, filling your heart and feeling the questions of life,

Every exhale, feeling self-acceptance and opening to answers and directions. . . .

Every inhale, filling your heart and feeling life,

Every exhale, feeling self-acceptance, innate wisdom, and clear direction in life,

Even as you read. . . .

11

Living Creatively

That there is nothing but energy, nothing but light, is commonplace knowledge. But how did light become so creative? Where did it get such a notion? Why should it be motivated to do any such thing? What light truly is is much more profound than a flash of heat and excitation. It is an infinite Genius, an Overwhelming, Mysterious, Blissful Purpose.

—ADI DA SAMRAJ, *SEE MY BRIGHTNESS FACE TO FACE*

Albert Einstein proved the primal connection between energy and matter. His formula $E=mc^2$ states that all matter consists of energy manifesting as mass. It further suggests that matter undergoes a constant process of slowly or quickly converting into energy, even as energy undergoes a reciprocal process of converting into matter.

The first practical applications of Einstein's insights went toward releasing the enormous quantities of energy held in certain forms of radioactive matter. This made sense since, beginning with the first wood fires and on through the development of candles and oil lamps, the invention of gunpowder, and all of the energy marvels of the Industrial and Nuclear Ages, people have long found ways to release the energy contained in matter. What a revelation to finally understand just what happens when we throw a log on a fire or a lump of coal into a furnace and things become warmer, brighter, or capable of doing more work—the material substance disappears as its mass transforms into energy, as m becomes E.

Fortunately, we have thus far managed to avoid using this "mass-into-energy" knowledge to do too much damage to our world; we can only hope that we will one day show as much facility, but much greater humility, moving in the opposite direction of Einstein's equation: the conversion of energy into matter. In order to do so we will need to comprehend the special nature of energy in living systems.

The first and second laws of thermodynamics describe the behavior of energy in nonorganic systems. The first law of thermodynamics tells us that we can neither create nor destroy energy. The total energy involved in any process (and in the universe) always remains constant. Energy may change form in the most complex ways but it never ceases to exist. The second law of thermodynamics describes an overall trend toward the decreasing order of energy. While the total energy involved in a process always remains constant, the amount of *usefully conserved* energy forever diminishes, as it dissipates through heat loss. When we cook food, for instance, much of the energy produced by our stove becomes absorbed first by the food and then again by our bodies as we eat (and thus remains usefully conserved). Some of the stove's energy, however, will radiate from the cooking pot as heat and then dissipate; it will no longer retain any useful organization.

When taken together, these two laws predict the slow degeneration of the universe, or *increasing entropy*, as an infinity of mechanical processes all steadily lose energy to disorganized heat and dissipation. At the macro level of burning stars and solar systems, the prediction of increasing entropy seems reasonable enough—though the universe has a fair amount of time remaining before it expires through "heat death." At the micro level of living cells and biological systems, however, we find that *decreasing entropy* simultaneously occurs: Living systems display the property of negative entropy, or a tendency toward increasing order of the system. Living systems grow even as they die, and for the whole system of planet Earth, life irrepressibly goes on even as it dissipates.

Consider a dead body. As it decomposes, the tiny organisms that feast upon the body conserve much of its energy, while some energy dissipates through the heat of decomposition. Overall we see a net gain in entropy, in accordance with the second law of thermodynamics.

A living body, however, transcends the law through its ability to reconfigure energy into organic growth. The body retains much of the energy presumed dissipated and converts that energy into useful mass. Here we see the evolutionary breakthrough of living systems: entropy reverses as energy becomes mass. As it moves through living systems energy gives rise to new order, greater complexity, and fresh material form. The energy of living systems serves as an infinitely creative force—becoming matter, becoming matter, becoming matter—always flowing against the tide of universal entropy.

Moreover, human beings show a unique capacity for the conscious influence of this creative force. We can learn to intentionally direct the moving energies that fill us and surround us and connect us to the world. As we suppress, express, or flow with our inward-moving energies, our bodies manifest as healthy or unhealthy flesh and blood. As our outward-moving energy fields expand or contract, our relationships turn loving or unloving. And as we pour our energy-selves into all that we do and have, we participate in the creation of the circumstances, events, and various things that make up our world—including our art, music, writings, crafts, gardens, homes, schools, consumer products, workplaces, religions, and governments.

All of human creation comes into existence via the regenerative powers of energy-in-motion. Our energy-alive minds and bodies function together (though often at cross-purposes) to give direction and form to life's creative imperative. As we perceive reality, respond to events, and engage in our lives, so energy moves through us and around us. As energy moves, so our bodies grow, our relationships develop, and our world creatively unfolds. As individuals we tend at all times either toward entropy (dissipating into death and disorder) or life (growing, evolving, transforming, and transcending). Whether consciously or unconsciously, we forever participate in the creation of our world through our moment-to-moment experience of energy-in-motion.

All living species reproduce. The ability to create new organisms from old gives life a key strategy in its eternal struggle with entropy. As organisms reproduce they use their material forms to direct the movement of energy into the manifestation of new life-infused matter. While the physical details differ greatly from species to species, the reproductive process essentially channels available energy into the conception, gestation, and birth of a new organism. Reproduction occurs only if energy moves to successfully quicken seed DNA and to fuel continuing growth.

In humans we see the movement of sexual energies prior to and independent of conception and reproduction. Most adolescents feel powerfully compelled by the sexual energies surging through their bodies long before and quite apart from any thoughts of propagating the race. They spend much of their teen years navigating the partly delicious, partly tormenting currents of sexual vibration. Adolescents feel urgently attracted to certain others, as if thrust together by nuclear-magnetic forces. They worry incessantly about their attractiveness or perceived lack thereof. They rush headlong into sexual and genital play with little thought to consequences and with little understanding of what it all means. They dance this oldest of all dances simply because they must, because as living creatures they must become channels for life's vital energies.

Meanwhile, we the hapless adults, former adolescents all, look upon our budding children with furrowed brows and gnashing teeth. We take legitimate concerns over unwanted pregnancies and sexually transmitted diseases and turn them into evil horrors come to prey on foolish sinners. We try to scare young people sexless. We badger them with "Just say no" and "Wait until marriage." While the advertising and entertainment industries broadcast an unremitting mantra of "Sex is good! Do it now! You'll be cool," we, the serious, ever naysaying authorities, counter with "Well, no, I mean, sex isn't *bad*, I guess, but, I mean, well, just don't do it." We wonder why they never listen.

Adolescents need to hear a simple, consistent, honest message that uplifts and beatifies their beautiful bodies; that extols the glories of sexual pleasure; that clearly lays out the benefits and risks of genital play, along with proven ways for reducing harm; that fully informs them about the moving energies of emotion, sex, and creativity; and that teaches them to effectively channel their awesome creative energies to make the world a better place. More than anything, we *all* need to understand and embrace our function as energy-channeling cocreators of this world.

Like sunlight and rain, the sexual-emotional energies flowing within and around us provide critical nourishment to our manifesting world. Energy, as it moves through human beings, becomes matter. Energy-in-motion serves as the raw material with which we participate in the cocreation of reality. Each of us succeeds or fails in life to the degree that we give form and direction to this creative force.

We make a huge mistake when we try to limit and suppress sexual energy. We fall into the ancient trap of thinking of sexual energy and genital play as existing primarily, if not exclusively, to further procreation. As a result we try to limit all feelings of sexual pleasure to one specific other, for one specific purpose. We ban all expressions of sexuality that fall outside the bounds of hetero-monogamy. We suppress, to our individual and collective detriment, the vital pulse of life, reducing to a mere trickle what should be an infinite river.

If we see humans as mere members of the animal kingdom, then the notion that we have sex for no other reason than causing pregnancy and passing on genes may make sense. When, however, we factor in human consciousness—the special mix of mind, heart, spirit, and awareness that defines and empowers our species—we cannot help but notice the limitations of such thinking. Sex has so much more to offer us than only making babies.

A strong current of sexual energy coursing through a body can heal wounds, can transform pathologies, can make a person feel lighter, brighter, and capable of doing more and better. Sexual energy can animate the artist's brush, can prompt the writer's words, can exalt the dancer's body, can fill the composer with joyful noise. Sexual energy provides the charismatic spark to inspire others, as well as the self-cauterizing fires of spiritual transformation. And, so important, sexual energy *feels good*. Free-flowing sexual energy gives us the simplest, most human of pleasures and, contrary to the crotchety rants of religious repressives and social prudes, feelings of pleasure provide far greater motivation toward right action than threats of shame, punishment, and eternal damnation. When people feel good they tend toward doing good.

When sexual energy flows between two or more people, it may lead to genital play and a mutual bathing in revitalizing pleasures. It may lead to a brand-new pregnancy. Or it may be channeled into a strong expansion of creativity within each person, providing the seed and the sustaining power to bring something new into the world. Active and productive relationships—with family members, coworkers, business partners, and best friends, or within athletic teams, artistic collaborations, and even most competitions—all have a current of sexual energy intercoursing among the participants, even if they never physically touch and even if they do not consciously entertain any thoughts of shared sexuality.

The eternal flux of sexual-creative energies occurs between all reasonably open people, regardless of gender, age, race, religion, marital status, sexual orientation, or unique station in life. Whenever two or more people come together to make something happen, sexual-creative energy flows to fill the void between them and to empower their actions. They have a sexual-energy-in-motion sharing experience. It can feel rote, forced, and uninspired, as for assembly line workers or test-taking students or sweatshop slaves. Or it can feel grand, juicy, and thrilling, as for jamming musicians and championship teams and emergency workers in the midst of a crisis.

To the extent that we sustain awareness of our energy-selves and stay open to the moving energies of others, then our lives grow rich with creative potential and valuable partners. We become comfortable with feeling sexual-creative energy with many others. We learn to appreciate the difference between genital play and creative play, and we experience both as divine pleasures. Though we may remain reserved regarding when and with whom we exchange bodily fluids, we easily and freely exchange creative energies with all willing partners.

Making full use of the sexual-creative energies available to us begins with the three practices of emotional flow: active acceptance, dynamic relaxation, and conscious connected breathing. As we feel so creative energies move. As we accept, relax into, and breathe with our current circumstances, we encourage free-flowing energy-in-motion and become more empowered in all that we do.

To these primary practices, we add one more: *creative choice.* As cocreators in this world we have an innate ability to give meaningful direction to the moving energies of life. We do this through our mental choices. We become open channels (or not) to energy-in-motion through the quality of our emotions. We direct available energy-in-motion toward specific manifestation through the quality of our minds. As we feel so energy moves. As we think so energy takes form.

Our minds comprise a wide variety of thoughts ranging from the banal and mundane to the grand and transcendental. A closely watched mind reveals an unceasing stream of images, voices, sounds, sensations, and memories usually flitting butterflylike from subject to subject. At other times the mind will lock in on various worries, obsessions, and fantasies and churn away for hours on end, unable to think of anything else. So many of our thoughts have no more significance than to provide fleeting distraction from external reality.

Some thoughts, however, really *matter*—they make material. We think, "I *am* . . . I *want* . . . I *must* . . . I *will* . . . I *choose* . . ."

and we turn our creative selves toward a specific end or object. Such thoughts focus our mental powers to direct and shape the flow of manifesting energy. These *manifesting thoughts* in effect tell energy where to go and what to do. They operate like subtle scripts to give express form and function to our creative energies.

Manifesting thoughts make choices; they have clear, decisive edges. The word *decide* comes from the Latin *decidere:* "to cut off." As the sculptor's chisel cuts off what does not belong in the final likeness, as the revising poet cuts through every unnecessary word, as the film editor cuts out unwanted footage, our most creative thoughts decide, delineate, determine, select, conclude, opt, intend, choose. Manifesting thoughts—decisions, goals, plans, invocations, affirmations, prayers, serious daydreams—all focus our creative energies by narrowing down a field of possibilities and settling on a single choice. As we cut off options and specify choice we intentionally direct the energy-in-motion of creativity.

We decide what we want, what we will do, or who we will become, and energy moves accordingly. We form a clear vision of the future and energy moves to make it so. We feel a strong desire for any outcome and energy moves to bring resolution. We consciously reach out to various others and energy moves into creative connection with all that we so touch.

We choose, energy moves, and so our lives unfold.

We cannot avoid our role as chooser-creators any more than we can avoid thinking. Every thought represents a choice at some level—to think about this rather than that; to give attention to *a* rather than *b*—and as we think we naturally form the mold through which our creative energies will flow. We can and must bring practical discipline to our mental processes so that we make conscious, reasoned choices that move creation in beneficent directions.

Each of us makes choices every day that positively or negatively alter the direction and outcome of circumstances and events. Our daily diet, our selection of friends, the place where we make our home, the work that we do, our avocations, our good and bad habits, the available colors in our palette, the specific steps in our dance, the words flowing onto each page of our story: whether consciously or not, we regularly make significant choices in all of these areas, even if we choose to let others choose for us. It behooves us to pay attention to our ever-flowing thoughts and gradually, with practice, to learn to commit our minds to positive creativity.

We cannot overstate the primal power of creative choice. No matter what the circumstances of our lives, we can always choose to think differently. We can *always* change our minds and thereby change our world. Even the helplessly destitute can choose their mental and emotional responses and give voice to the desire for something better. Even the most tightly shackled prisoner or desperately ill patient can choose a free-flowing pattern of breathing and thus elicit freer-flowing thoughts and feelings. We always have significant life-altering choices available to us, however trapped and powerless we have come to feel.

Moreover, all the creative force flowing from any one person becomes magnified when people choose in concert. The collective choices of families, groups, communities, nations, and leagues of nations generate progressively greater effects—too often, it seems, for the worse. In the last few decades of the twentieth century the destructive effects of what should be our creative powers have become the stuff of daily headlines. Thousands of species have gone extinct because of self-serving human choices. The planet's forests have suffered greatly from acid rain and overcutting. The oceans have likewise suffered from various pollutants, overfishing, and a slow warming trend. Humans have scattered biodestructive poisons everywhere, tainting soil, water, and air. Our foolish choices have even altered the planetary atmosphere, effectively making sunlight toxic and ushering in an age of perilous climate change.

Humanity finds itself in the undeserved position of having dominion over most of life's creatures and processes. This does not mean, as too many believe, that we should become the chest-thumping alpha species of the planet, brutally dominating anything or anyone that gets in our way. It means that whether through chance, evolution, or divine intent, we have the power to fundamentally affect, for better and worse, 'till entropy do us part, the direction and quality of life unfolding. The tiller of planetary evolution rests firmly in our collective hands; as humanity chooses so the world turns.

So choose wisely and teach your children to do the same. Understand your destiny as cocreator and revel in the emotional, sexual, and creative energies that move through you and surround you. Actively accept the people, circumstances, and events in your life. Relax. Breathe free. Practice creation.

Before beginning the Intention Breath practice, identify a current goal or intention in your life. State it in a positive form, beginning with "I will . . ."; for example, "I will find a better job this week," "I will fully forgive and accept my father," "I will begin and stick with this new exercise regimen," "I will become a more loving person."

—◄○►—

Intention Breath

Now, even as you read, bring attention to the movement of your breath.

Breathe in deeply through your nose, filling your torso,

And breathe out through the mouth in a long, soft, gentle sssshhhh. . . .

Now, continuing with this breathing, feel or sense or imagine that as you inhale

Energy flows into and fills your heart, the center of your chest,

And as you breathe out the energy radiates out from the heart

In all directions, sssshhhh. . . .

Inhaling, your heart fills with love-energy,

Exhaling, love-energy radiates out from the heart, as light from a star, sssshhhh. . . .

Continue with several long, slow, gentle heart breaths. . . .

Now, as you inhale, filling your heart, state your intention, and then,

As you exhale, radiating from your heart, feel deep and overflowing gratitude,

As if your intention had already manifested. . . .

Every inhale, filling your heart and affirming your intention,

Every exhale, radiating from your heart,

Feeling deeply grateful for life unfolding. . . .

Every inhale, filling your heart and feeling all that you will.

Every exhale, feeling gratitude for all that is,

Every inhale, filling your heart and feeling creation,

Every exhale, feeling deeply grateful for all that is,

Even as you read. . . .

Epilogue

An old story tells of a monkey who comes across a caged bird. Thinking of dinner, the monkey reaches through the bars of the cage and grabs the bird. Yet his fist, now clenched tightly around his prize, can no longer squeeze back through the bars. The monkey, unwilling to simply let go, eventually dies, caught in a trap of his own making.

The monkey's dilemma—how to let go when remaining clenched seems so necessary—resembles our own problems with emotional suppression, relational inheritance, and social viruses. If we accept that we have become riddled with the contracted emotional energies of the past, then how do we let them all go? If we observe ourselves chronically clenching and stifling emotional energy, then how can we do otherwise? How do we free ourselves from a lifetime of emotional baggage? How do we reverse lifelong emotional habits?

We might imagine our friend the monkey as a modern seeker on the path to enlightenment. He could tackle his feelings of being trapped in any number of ways. He could berate himself for his misplaced desires and his addiction to birds. He could spend hours and hours analyzing his past in an attempt to clarify the process that brought him to his current condition. He could blame his parents for his unfulfilled hunger and his compulsion to overachieve. He could worry over his genetic makeup and whether he was doomed from birth by bird-craving genes. He could pray to God to "take this bird away" from him. He could see a doctor who might recommend surgically removing the hand or perhaps trying liposuction.

Or he could just release the bird.

You can just release your emotions. At this moment you can let your emotional energies move; at this moment you can flow; at this moment you can. It will help if you learn to let events and circumstances happen as they happen, if you let your body relax, if you let your breathing move freely, if, at this moment, you clearly choose to let go. It will surely help if you diligently practice letting go, if you seriously work at it, if you make letting go, letting flow, and letting be the central themes of your existence.

But it always comes back to the monkey's simple choice: keep holding on or let go now. Keep holding on. Or let go. Now.

Notes on Continuing Practice

1. This book encourages "breathing practice" as a constant awareness in your life. Make a commitment to conscious intentional breathing at all times and places. Breathing, when practiced with active acceptance, dynamic relaxation, and creative intention, can become a way of feeling alive in every moment and of freely flowing with the forever flux of circumstances and events.

2. You may also wish to practice breathing in a more meditative pose. At such times take care that your back remains relatively straight—while remembering that the back has natural curves. If sitting in a chair move your buttocks to the outer edge of the seat, away from the chair back, since the backs of most chairs encourage slumping. If sitting cross-legged on the floor try placing a small pillow beneath your buttocks. If lying down it can help to elevate the knees.

3. Touching the tip of your tongue to the roof of your mouth enhances an important inward flow of energy.

4. Chronic contracted breathing narrows the range of both the inhale and exhale. If you never fully exhale then you have no room in your lungs for a full inhale. If you never fully inhale then the overall capacity of your respiratory system (includ-

ing lungs, diaphragm, rib cage, and all of the connecting muscles of the region) diminishes. You eventually become structurally unable to take a complete breath, no matter how hard you try.

5. We use the hushing breath (sssshhhh . . .) to effect a full exhale. By "sounding out" the breath until empty you create the space for a full, vigorous, body-initiated inhale. Continuing practice gradually expands the respiratory system toward full capacity. Both inhaling and exhaling will become longer, deeper, and slower, even as the immediate feeling of breathing ranges from quiet pleasure to tingling joy.

6. In the beginning use the hushing breath throughout your day and as often as circumstances allow. Especially notice those people and situations that tend to inhibit your breathing. Come awake at such times, remembering the breath, moving energy, and feeling acceptance. Do a few long, slow hushing breaths to set the pattern of full release leading to full reception.

7. After sufficient time and practice you will have retrained your breathing to a fuller, more feeling, and more life-enhancing pattern. You will mostly breathe in and out through your nose, in accordance with the body's design. You can always do a few hushing breaths whenever you feel yourself contracting.

8. When doing heart breathing, consciously involve your entire torso in every breath. Even as you focus your awareness in the center of your chest, your belly, diaphragm, rib cage, and collarbones should all move with both the inhale and exhale. Think of your torso as a balloon: every inhale, your torso expands simultaneously, lower and upper, front, back, and sides; every exhale, your torso shrinks simultaneously, lower and upper, front, back, and sides.

9. Let your breath become a reminder to return to the heart, to rest peacefully in the heart, to dwell in the house of the Lord— the heart—forever. Everything improves with heart breathing. When centered in the heart you come into more meaningful

connection with people and circumstances. You naturally think more clearly, your body works better, you have greater access to inner wisdom, and you flow more easily with life's changes.

10. As gentle, flowing heart breathing becomes natural and easy, make yourself a forever fountain of love-energy. Give away, give away, give away.

11. For further insight into breathing and more breathing practices, see my earlier book, *Breathing: Expanding Your Power and Energy* (Santa Fe: Bear & Company, 1990).

12. I strongly encourage exploring the brilliant teachings of Adi Da Samraj. In the past thirty years he has created a vast library of his unique wisdom, as well as a vibrant international community. Visit the Web site www.adidam.org, or call: (800) 524-4941.

About the Author

Michael Sky is a holistic healer, teacher, writer, and editor. Since 1976 he has maintained a private practice as a therapist and bodyworker, focusing on breath, life energy, and the resolution of suppressed emotions. He has traveled throughout the United States and Japan leading workshops in the exploration of breathing, bodywork, ritual, and the effective practice of partnership. He is the author of *Breathing* (Bear & Company, 1990), a definitive book on the use of breath for therapeutic and spiritual benefits, and is the managing editor of the *NAPRA ReView,* a bimonthly magazine serving the body/mind/spirit marketplace. He lives with his wife and daughter on a small green island in the Pacific Northwest.

To contact the author:

Michael Sky

12 Opal Commons

Eastsound, WA 98245

sky@rockisland.com